Evaluating
School Superintendents

Evaluating
School Superintendents

A Guide to Employing Processes and Practices That Are Fair and Effective

Michael F. DiPaola, Tracey L. Schneider, and Steven R. Staples

ROWMAN & LITTLEFIELD
Lanham • Boulder • New York • London

Published by Rowman & Littlefield
An imprint of The Rowman & Littlefield Publishing Group, Inc.
4501 Forbes Boulevard, Suite 200, Lanham, Maryland 20706
www.rowman.com

6 Tinworth Street, London SE11 5AL, United Kingdom

British Library Cataloguing in Publication Information Available

Library of Congress Cataloging-in-Publication Data

Names: DiPaola, Michael F., 1947- author. | Schneider, Tracey L., author. |
   Staples, Steven R., author.
Title: Evaluating school superintendents : a guide to employing fair and
   effective processes and practices / Michael F. DiPaola, Tracey L.
   Schneider and Steven R. Staples.
Description: Lanham : Rowman & Littlefield, [2019] | Includes
   bibliographical references and index. | Summary: "This book outlines the
   rationale for a regular, systematic, comprehensive evaluation of school
   district superintendents"— Provided by publisher.
Identifiers: LCCN 2019016679 (print) | LCCN 2019022204 (ebook) | ISBN
   9781475846942 (cloth) | ISBN 9781475846959 (pbk.)
Subjects: LCSH: School superintendents—Rating of—United States. | School
   superintendents—Evaluation. | School districts—Management.
Classification: LCC LB2831.762 .D55 2019 (print) | LCC LB2831.762 (ebook)
   | DDC 371.2/011—dc23
LC record available at https://lccn.loc.gov/2019016679
LC ebook record available at https://lccn.loc.gov/2019022204

Contents

Foreword

During my service as the Secretary of Education for Virginia, there was a strong emphasis on encouraging and supporting school improvement. As I did that work, it became evident to me that lasting school improvement, the kind that outlived staff turnover and leadership changes, required a focus on the entire school district, not just a single school or two. And the real key to district-level work was strong, capable leadership at the top; strong superintendents can make a huge difference in the performance of schools.

But frequent turnover in this critical position is too prevalent, and the process of evaluating superintendents is too often a contributing factor. Poorly done evaluations can lead to mistrust, hard feelings, and reduced communication between boards and superintendents. Conversely, quality superintendent evaluations can have a positive impact that helps develop the strength and stability of leadership we see in higher-performing school districts. That's why I wholeheartedly endorse this book's approach to superintendent evaluation. Knowing the authentic experiences of these authors and having watched Steve Staples travel the Commonwealth to help mentor and develop strong superintendent leaders, I am pleased to add my support to this work. Read it and use it to build a quality evaluation approach for superintendents that can enhance the superintendent-board relationship and bring a commitment to school improvement that really matters . . . and lasts.

Anne Holton, Former Virginia Secretary of Education
Visiting Professor of Education Policy, George Mason University

Preface

Superintendent Evaluation

The role of the superintendent has evolved with the dramatic changes in the landscape of public education during the past two decades. School accountability and reform movements have contributed to the role complexity and array of performance expectations of school superintendents. Despite the key role and responsibilities of the superintendent, the performance evaluation of the superintendent has continued not to be a high priority. Yet a conceptually sound and properly implemented evaluation system for the superintendent is a vital component of an effective school system.

Regardless of how well educational programs may be designed, the programs are only as effective as the people who implement and support them. Thus, a rational relationship exists between personnel and programs: effective people ensure effective programs. If program effectiveness is important and if personnel are necessary for effective programming, then a conceptually sound and properly implemented evaluation system for all employees, including the superintendent, is essential.

The purpose of this book is to provide guidelines to conduct a high-quality, research-based evaluation of a school superintendent and snapshot of contemporary practices of superintendent evaluation across the United States. Like the *Superintendent Evaluation Handbook* (DiPaola and Stronge, 2003) published more than a decade and a half ago, it explores the important issue of evaluation for the superintendent, addressing the aspects of that process that make it unique.

HOW IS THIS BOOK ORGANIZED?

This introductory chapter addresses the issue of evaluating specialized educational personnel, like the superintendent, in a manner that will ensure fairness to the individual educator as well as to the school district and community. The focus of all evaluations, including those that have a summative element, should be on improvement. Evaluation is merely a means to an end. Improving individual performance in order to provide quality services and programs to students is the ultimate purpose of evaluation. The intent of this book is to facilitate that effort.

Subsequent chapters are organized as outlined in table 0.1.

Table 0.1.   Key Steps in Understanding and Designing the Superintendent's Performance Evaluation System

Chapter	Focus
2 Background and History	• What is the history of superintendent evaluation? • What evaluation models can be considered for superintendent evaluation?
3 Current Status of Superintendent Evaluation State by State	• The existing state policies that require/govern superintendent evaluations & their impact on practice. • What are the consequences of not having a clear set of policies/procedures?
4 Performance Standards	• What are the superintendent's major roles and responsibilities upon which the evaluation will be based?
5 Documenting the Superintendent's Performance	• How will performance of the superintendent's job be documented? • How well is the superintendent expected to perform?
6 Implementing the Superintendent's Performance Evaluation	• What is needed in terms of policy, procedures, and training for successful implementation of a superintendent evaluation system?
7 Where Do We Go from Here?	• How do all the pieces fit? • Where do we go from here?

In addition to the chapters, accompanying appendices that contain numerous forms, formats, tools, and techniques intended to make the practical tasks of developing and implementing a quality superintendent evaluation system easier are included. Moreover, in developing this book, the overarching goal has been to advocate for and facilitate the design of a fair and comprehensive system for superintendent evaluation that:

- Connects the superintendent's performance to school board and school district goals and objectives
- Holds superintendents responsible for high but realistic expectations for performance
- Is professionalizing for the superintendent
- Provides opportunities for growth
- Can be objectively assessed using appropriate data sources
- Is practical to implement

REFERENCE

DiPaola, M. F., and Stronge, J. H. (2003). *The superintendent evaluation handbook.* Lanham, MD: Scarecrow Press.

Chapter One

Superintendent Evaluation

Getting Started

This introductory chapter addresses the questions:

- Why is superintendent evaluation an important issue?
- What particular challenges are posed by superintendent evaluation?
- What are criteria for superintendent evaluation?

WHY IS SUPERINTENDENT EVALUATION AN IMPORTANT ISSUE?

Despite the fact that proper evaluation of the superintendent of schools is fundamentally important, this aspect of performance evaluation is frequently neglected. "The fundamental purpose of personnel evaluations must be to help provide effective services to students" (Joint Committee on Standards for Educational Evaluation [JCSEE], 2009, p. 3). Personnel evaluations in education historically have focused primarily on classroom teachers and, in more recent years, on principals, counselors, and other building-based personnel.

In 1980, the American Association of School Administrators (AASA) and the National School Boards Association (NSBA) issued a joint statement calling for formal evaluations of superintendents (AASA, 1980), yet in the intervening years little systemic progress was made. The lack of systemic progress continues despite federal accountability and reform initiatives, like the Every Student Succeeds Act, that shift the focus of reform efforts from the building-based level to the district-based level (Whitehouse, 2017). While building-based positions are vital to school success, we can no longer afford to overlook the performance evaluation of the school system's CEO—the superintendent.

Whether we are discussing the evaluation of the superintendent, the classroom teacher, or another position, the need is basic: a thoughtful, thorough, and fair evaluation based on performance and designed to encourage improvement in both the person being evaluated and the school. Nonetheless, the job of the superintendent and, consequently, her or his evaluation, are unique within the school system.

Regarding the work of the superintendent, the position is an amalgam of roles and responsibilities, including to:

- Provide instructional leadership
- Promote student progress
- Recommend policy to the board
- Implement board policy
- Plan strategically
- Set and implement goals
- Manage district resources
- Hire, supervise, support, and evaluate staff
- Communicate and engage with all constituents
- Set the tone for the district
- Be politically astute and work with local political officers
- Implement applicable state and federal laws
- Work effectively with employee groups
- Understand collective bargaining (Callan and Levinson, 2011)

In essence, the superintendent personifies the aspirations and responsibilities of the entire organization.

Despite the formal, wide-ranging responsibilities, when it comes to performance assessment, the superintendent's evaluation is too frequently conducted through a highly informal process based more on impressions than real data (Peterson, 1989) and based more on politics than actual performance. Moreover, she or he is the only employee in the entire organization who is supervised by multiple evaluators, all of whom typically are community members, unfamiliar with the complexities of running a school system and untrained in the evaluation of professional educators.

Regardless of local board of education governance structure, board members face regular turnover and are necessarily influenced by the politics of either election or appointment to the board. Moving beyond, or at least recognizing and accounting for the unique challenges of superintendent evaluation, is essential.

The success of the superintendent and, ultimately, the success of the school system are inextricably linked. If the superintendent of schools is to receive a fair evaluation, and if the evaluation is to contribute to her or his success and to the overall effectiveness of the school system as a whole, then special consideration must be given to designing, developing, and implementing a comprehensive and quality performance evaluation system.

WHAT PARTICULAR CHALLENGES ARE POSED BY SUPERINTENDENT EVALUATION?

Designing and implementing a sound performance evaluation system for the superintendent is a comprehensive and complex undertaking that we explore in more depth in subsequent chapters. A brief review of four of the more practical problems that face boards of education in implementing an evaluation system appropriate for the superintendent serves as a foundation for further discussion:

* Having multiple evaluators
* Political influences
* Clarifying performance expectations
* Documenting performance

Multiple Evaluators: Multiple Expectations

One of the factors that makes the evaluation of the superintendent unique is the lack of a single supervisor determining performance expectations and assessing the quality of performance. The utility standard of the JCSEE requires "that persons with appropriate expertise and credibility conduct the evaluations" (2009, p. 6). Yet typically, the superintendent is evaluated by all members of the board, most of whom are lay members of the community who have uneven or a lack of training in performance evaluation (MacPhail-Wilcox and Forbes, 1990).

Consequently, when five, seven, or nine members of the school board evaluate the superintendent, the resulting evaluation can be a conglomerate of conflicting perspectives—both in terms of expectations and performance. With this practice, one of two approaches frequently emerges.

1. The diverse opinions regarding the superintendent's performance get bandied about by the board members until a general consensus, an averaging of the varied opinions, or a compromise emerges.

2. The school board simply compiles all of the ratings and comments of individual board members and presents the composite list to the superintendent as the final evaluation.

Neither process serves the superintendent, the board, or the community well. With the first approach—evaluation by averaging—the feedback is too frequently general in nature and lacking in specificity. In the second approach—evaluation by composite—the feedback is too specific, offering conflicting advice, priorities, and directives.

Both methods fail to produce constructive results. Instead, they result in a general "feel good" approach when things are perceived to be going well, or acrimony among the board members and between the board and the superintendent when things are not going well. All too often the resulting evaluation is not constructive and contains threatening or demoralizing characteristics. Thus, both approaches are counterproductive to the success of the board, the superintendent, and, ultimately, the primary clients of the school system—the students.

The Role of Politics

Underlying the multiplicity of board member expectations and perspectives is the inevitable influence of politics. Though state laws often try to remove the role of partisan politics in local board of education elections or appointments, such issues are always present below the surface, influencing the fairness of the superintendent evaluation process.

Despite these efforts, the superintendent role is inextricably tied to politics. Different political perspectives lead to frequent changes and turnover in board membership. This rotation and the continual introduction of new membership, new personalities, new political perspectives, and new educational and evaluation philosophies make development of consistent and meaningful evaluation criteria extremely difficult (Mayo and McCartney, 2004). Superintendents are forced to adapt to the role expectations of the board, the community that elects the board (Björk and Gurley, 2005), or the political government official that appoints the board.

The inevitable political influence holds true regardless of whether the superintendent is elected or appointed. Elected superintendents report directly to the public. Though appointed superintendents technically report to the board of education, the board of education is the elected or appointed representative of the public. Thus, elected or appointed, superintendents report to the public, either directly or indirectly, and serve as political figures (Schneider, 2019).

Performance Expectations

Another problem often plaguing the superintendent evaluation process is the absence of clearly defined job expectations and performance goals. For a new superintendent, often the assumption is that the recent selection process clarified the expectations; for a continuing superintendent, a general understanding based on past practice frequently is used. Few superintendents receive suggestions for professional growth during an evaluation, and meaningful evaluations should address both strengths and weaknesses (Candoli, Cullen, and Stufflebeam, 1997).

A better process for both the new and the continuing superintendent is to jointly establish with the board clear and specific goals for the organization and the expectations of the superintendent in fulfilling those goals (Schaffer, 1999). By discussing and collaboratively establishing mutually agreeable organizational goals and performance targets, the job of the superintendent can more readily be translated into job responsibilities with appropriate performance indicators and standards for job performance.

This collaborative process clearly requires input from both the school board and the superintendent, who ultimately is responsible for carrying out the daily performance of job expectations. Only by a joint process of defining responsibilities and standards of performance can there be clear direction for the school system, the evaluation process, and the superintendent being evaluated.

Documentation of Performance

Documenting the superintendent's job performance should also be considered a collaborative process, with both the board and the superintendent gathering and assessing performance data. However, the critical issue is the need to rely on tangible, objective ways of knowing how well the superintendent performs.

When the superintendent's evaluation is based merely on supposition drawn from informal sources or flavored by the most recent set of circumstances and events, the evidence upon which decisions are made is superficial. An informal process for documenting performance can easily result in numerous problems, including:

• Perceptions skewed by a few vocal advocates or complainants
• Performance reviews based on anecdotal, partial evidence
• Evaluations unrelated to measures of success or achievement of organizational goals
• Evaluations based on unreasonable reactions to negative test score data

- A false sense of security regarding progress
- Decisions uninformed by results
- The absence of clear direction for continuous improvement and future direction

Rather than rely on poor or partial evidence for documenting performance, we advocate a system that builds upon multiple sources of performance evidence, including goal accomplishment, self-assessment, informal observation, client feedback, and analysis of artifacts. The use of multiple data sources such as these can more accurately reflect the multifaceted job dimensions of the superintendent's role and success in fulfilling that role.

WHAT ARE RELEVANT CRITERIA FOR SUPERINTENDENT EVALUATION?

At its inception, any personnel evaluation system should properly address the standards developed by the JCSEE (2009): propriety, utility, feasibility, and accuracy. Although there may be unique aspects to the nature of the superintendent's role, the position has in common, with all educational personnel, the need for fair, job-relevant, and meaningful evaluations.

Unfortunately, as with teachers and administrators, superintendents have suffered from numerous systemic problems with the state-of-the-art personnel evaluation (Stronge, 2003). The JCSEE (2009) stated that personnel evaluation in education has "too often done poorly with detrimental outcomes" (p. xix), despite the centrality of the process.

Dominant criticisms of personnel evaluation practices include:

- Lack of constructive feedback
- Failure to recognize and reinforce outstanding service
- Dividing rather than unifying collective efforts to educate students

For evaluation to be beneficial to the superintendent and the school system, traditional problems such as those noted earlier must be resolved.

One ready solution is to develop and implement performance evaluation systems that adhere to the Personnel Evaluation Standards. A brief overview of how the four basic standards can be incorporated into superintendent evaluation is provided in table 1.1. A detailed discussion of each of the four sets of standards follows.

Table 1.1. Application of Personnel Evaluation Standards to Superintendent Evaluation

Standards	Description of the Standards	Application to Superintendent Evaluation
Propriety Standards . . .	"are intended to ensure that a personnel evaluation will be conducted legally, ethically, and with due regard for the welfare of the evaluatee and those involved in the evaluation."	• ensure that the superintendent's evaluation adheres to legal and ethical standards • ensure that the work of the superintendent serves the best interests of the schools and students
Utility Standards . . .	"are intended to guide evaluations so that they **will** be informative, timely, and influential."	• provide for an informative and useful superintendent evaluation process • provide evaluation feedback that guides improvement and delivery of high-quality services
Feasibility Standards . . .	"are intended to guide personnel evaluation systems so that they are as easy to implement as possible, efficient in their use of time and resources, adequately funded, and viable from a political standpoint."	• provide for a practical superintendent evaluation process in light of social, political, and government forces and constraints
Accuracy Standards . . .	"must be technically adequate and as complete as possible to allow sound judgments and decisions to be made. The evaluation methodology should be appropriate for the purpose of the evaluation and the evaluatees being evaluated and the context in which they work."	• offer a basis for determining the soundness of the evaluation in assessing the superintendent's performance

Source: JCSEE, *The Personnel Evaluation Standards*, 2009.

Propriety Standards

Propriety Standards require "that a personnel evaluation be conducted legally, ethically, and with due regard for the welfare of evaluatee and those involved in the evaluation" (JCSEE, 2009, p. 6). Ultimately the superintendent's evaluation should establish a system that directly supports a primary principle—schools exist to serve students.

For ease of reference, a number indicating the specific standard follows the first letter of the category of standards (e.g., P for propriety). The seven Propriety Standards include:

- P1 Service Orientation—Personnel evaluations should promote sound education, fulfillment of institutional missions, and effective performance of job responsibilities, so that the educational needs of students, community, and society are met.
- P2 Appropriate Policies and Procedures—Guidelines for personnel evaluations should be recorded and provided to the evaluatee in policy statements, negotiated agreements, and/or personnel evaluation manuals, so that evaluations are consistent, equitable, and fair.
- P3 Access to Evaluation Information—Access to evaluation information should be limited to the persons with established legitimate permission to review and use the information, so that confidentiality is maintained and privacy protected.
- P4 Interactions with Evaluatees—The evaluator should respect human dignity and act in a professional, considerate, and courteous manner, so that the evaluatee's self-esteem, motivation, professional reputations, performance, and attitude toward personnel evaluation are enhanced or, at least, not needlessly damaged.
- P5 Balanced Evaluation—Personnel evaluations should provide information that identifies both strengths and weaknesses, so that strengths can be built upon and weaknesses addressed.
- P6 Conflict of Interest—Existing and potential conflicts of interest should be identified and dealt with openly and honestly, so that they do not compromise the evaluation process and results.
- P7 Legal Viability—Personnel evaluations should meet the requirements of all federal, state, and local laws, as well as case law, contracts, collective bargaining agreements, affirmative action policies, and local board policies and regulations or institutional statutes or bylaws, so that evaluators can successfully conduct fair, efficient, and responsible personnel evaluations.

Utility Standards

"Utility Standards are intended to guide evaluations so that they will be informative, timely, and influential" (JCSEE, 2009, p. 69). As with other educators' evaluations, the evaluation of superintendents should inform decision makers regarding goal achievement. While our interests in this book revolve around the superintendent's evaluation, the collective evaluations of all employees should relate individual performance to the overarching organizational goals.

This concept of utility is illuminated in six specific standards:

- U1 Constructive Orientation—Personnel evaluations should be constructive, so that they not only help institutions develop human resources but also encourage and assist those evaluated to provide excellent services in accordance with the institution's mission statements and goals.
- U2 Defined Uses—Both the users and intended uses of a personnel evaluation should be identified at the beginning of the evaluation so that the evaluation can address appropriate questions and issues.
- U3 Evaluator Qualifications—The evaluation system should be developed, implemented, and managed by persons with the necessary qualifications, skills, training, and authority, so that evaluation reports are properly conducted, respected, and used.
- U4 Explicit Criteria—Evaluators should identify and justify the criteria used to interpret and judge evaluatee performance, so that the basis for interpretation and judgment provide a clear and defensible rationale for results.
- U5 Functional Reporting—Reports should be clear, timely, accurate, and germane, so that they are of practical value to the evaluatee and other appropriate audiences.
- U6 Professional Development—Personnel evaluations should inform users and evaluatees of areas in need of professional development, so that all educational personnel can better address the institution's mission and goals, fulfill their roles and responsibilities, and meet the needs of students.

Feasibility Standards

The Feasibility Standards state that evaluation systems should be "as easy to implement as possible, efficient in their use of time and resources, adequately funded, and viable from a political standpoint" (JCSEE, 2009, p. 99). An evaluation system that satisfies the Feasibility Standards will be applicable specifically to superintendents while, at the same time, it will be sensitive to the practical issues related to proper evaluation within the school system.

The Feasibility category includes three specific standards:

- F1 Practical Procedures—Personnel evaluation procedures should be practical, so that they produce the needed information in efficient, nondisruptive ways.
- F2 Political Viability—Personnel evaluations should be planned and conducted with the anticipation of questions from evaluatees and others with a legitimate right to know, so that their questions can be addressed and their cooperation obtained.

- F3 Fiscal Viability—Adequate time and resources should be provided for personnel evaluation activities, so that evaluation can be effectively implemented, the results fully communicated, and appropriate follow-up activities identified.

Accuracy Standards

Accuracy Standards state, "Personnel evaluations must be technically adequate and as complete as possible to allow sound judgments and decisions to be made. The evaluation methodology should be appropriate for the purpose of the evaluation and the evaluatees being evaluated and the context in which they work" (JCSEE, 2009, p. 115).

The eleven standards within the Accuracy category can be summarized as follows:

- A1 Validity Orientation—The selection, development, and implementation of personnel evaluations should ensure that the interpretations made about the performance of the evaluatee are valid and not open to misinterpretation.
- A2 Defined Expectations—The qualifications, role, and performance expectations of the evaluatee should be clearly defined, so that the evaluator can determine the evaluation data and information needed to ensure validity.
- A3 Analysis of Context—Contextual variables that influence performance should be identified, described, and recorded, so that they can be considered when interpreting an evaluatee's performance.
- A4 Documented Purposes and Procedures—The evaluation purposes and procedures, both planned and actual, should be documented, so that they can be clearly explained and justified.
- A5 Defensible Information—The information collected for personnel evaluations should be defensible, so that the information can be reliably and validly interpreted.
- A6 Reliable Information—Personnel evaluation procedures should be chosen or developed and implemented to assure reliability, so that the information obtained will provide consistent indications of the evaluatee's performance.
- A7 Systematic Data Control—The information collected, processed, and reported about evaluatees should be systematically reviewed, corrected as appropriate, and kept secure, so that accurate judgments about the evaluatee's performance can be made and appropriate levels of confidentiality maintained.

- A8 Bias Identification and Management—Personnel evaluations should be free of bias, so that interpretations of the evaluatee's qualifications or performance are valid.
- A9 Analysis of Information—The information collected for personnel evaluations should be systematically and accurately analyzed, so that the purposes of the evaluation are effectively achieved.
- A10 Justified Conclusions—The evaluative conclusions about the evaluatee's performance should be explicitly justified, so that evaluatees and others with a legitimate right to know can have confidence in them.
- A11 Meta-Evaluation—Personnel evaluation systems should be examined periodically using these and other appropriate standards, so that mistakes are prevented or detected and promptly corrected, and sound personnel evaluation practices are developed and maintained over time.

REFERENCES

American Association of School Administrators. (1980). *Evaluating the superintendent.* Arlington, VA: Author.

Björk, L. G., and Gurley, D. K. (2005). Superintendent as educational statements and political strategist. In L. G. Björk and T. J. Kowalski (Eds.), *The contemporary superintendent: Preparation, practice, and development* (pp. 45–69). Thousand Oaks, CA: Corwin Press.

Callan, M. F., and Levinson, W. (2011). *Achieving success for new and aspiring superintendents: A practical guide.* Thousand Oaks, CA: Corwin Press.

Candoli, I. C., Cullen, K., and Stufflebeam, D. L. (1997). *Superintendent performance evaluation: Current practice and directions for improvement.* Boston: Kluwer Academic Publishers.

Joint Committee on Standards for Educational Evaluation. (2009). *The personnel evaluation standards: How to assess systems for evaluating educators* (second ed.). Thousand Oaks, CA: Corwin Press.

MacPhail-Wilcox, B., and Forbes, R. (1990). *Administrator evaluation handbook: How to design a system of administrative evaluation.* Bloomington, IN: Phi Delta Kappa.

Mayo, C. R., and McCartney, G. P. (2004). School superintendents' evaluations: Effective and results-based? *ERS Spectrum*, 22(1), 19–33.

Peterson, D. (1989). *Superintendent evaluation.* Eugene, OR: ERIC Clearing House on Educational Management (ERIC Digest Series Number EA 42).

Schaffer, F. M. (1999). The processes and practices of superintendent performance evaluation in a mid-Atlantic state. Doctoral dissertation, University of Maryland (UMI Dissertation Services, UMI No. 99258:31).

Schneider, T. L. (2019). A state-level superintendent evaluation policy analysis (Doctoral dissertation). Retrieved from ProQuest Dissertations and Theses (10977630).

Stronge, J. H. (2003). Evaluating educational specialists. In T. Kellaghan and D. Stufflebeam (Eds.), *The international handbook of educational evaluation*, 671–93. Boston, MA: Kluwer Academic Press.

Whitehouse, E. (2017, July/August). What the Every Student Succeeds Act means for state education leaders. The Current State [e-newsletter of The Council of State Governments]. Retrieved from http://www.csg.org/pubs/capitolideas/enews/cs46_1.aspx.

Chapter Two

Background and History

Since its inception, the role of the school superintendent has evolved in response to changes in the goals of public education and the needs of school boards. Superintendents are the educational experts that guide lay boards of education in the governance of school districts and are the chief executive officers of districts.

The nature of the relationships between superintendents and school boards, as well as the perceived effectiveness of superintendents, also has evolved. Stufflebeam (1995) called the superintendency "one of the most complex and challenging leadership roles in American society" (p. 159).

In this chapter we provide a historical background and models of evaluation. In particular, we address the following questions:

- How has the role of the superintendent evolved since its inception?
- What are the critical leadership skills for an effective superintendent?
- What is the history of superintendent evaluation?
- What is the relationship between performance expectations of the superintendent and evaluative criteria used to assess performance?
- What are the purposes of superintendent evaluation?
- What are the merits of different models of superintendent evaluation?

HOW HAS THE ROLE OF THE SUPERINTENDENT
CHANGED SINCE ITS INCEPTION?

The first superintendent was appointed in 1837 when the board of education in Buffalo, New York, determined that "a full-time leader was needed to carry out the policies initiated by the board" (cited in Carter and Cunningham,

1997, p. 22). Later that same year, Louisville, Kentucky, followed and appointed a superintendent of public schools.

Early generations of superintendents were appointed to solve administrative problems confronting the growth in numbers and in sizes of public schools. Teachers alone were responsible for what happened in classrooms during the nineteenth century, and school curricula remained static.

In 1874 the Kalamazoo case (*Stuart v. School District No. 1 of Village of Kalamazoo*), which granted local school boards the right to tax property owners to support education, provided another reason to have a central, top-level administrator. Hence, by the end of that century, superintendents were common in cities, where they assisted lay school boards in the operation of schools.

The twentieth century emerged with a debate between classicists and modernists concerning curriculum content (Potter, 1967). School populations were growing, and virtually all the states had adopted compulsory attendance laws. School boards looked to superintendents to take active roles as the expert educators in the district, guiding curricular decisions and instructional practices.

By the mid-1930s, improved roads and motor buses facilitated a trend to consolidate and dramatically reduce the number of one-room schools. The expansion of student enrollment, experiments in curriculum, and legislative enactments affecting curriculum all contributed to a more complex role for school leaders. Consequently, organizational complexity led to a role for superintendents that was primarily "administrative" in nature.

Moreover, scientific management practices were adopted from the private sector. Boards became policymaking bodies and school superintendents ran school districts day to day. During ensuing decades, boards wanted expert managers to lead their school districts. Carter and Cunningham called this "the era of the four B's: bonds, buses, budgets, and buildings" (1997, p. 23).

An earned high school diploma, uncommon prior to World War II, became a reality for almost 50 percent of the population by the end of the 1950s. During that decade, a significant event, the launch of *Sputnik* in 1957, shaped the evolving superintendency. This achievement of the Soviet Union during the Cold War era changed public expectations of public schools and generated national legislation that dramatically impacted curriculum.

The Elementary and Secondary Education Act of 1965 (ESEA) was originally passed as part of the War on Poverty campaign. The original goal of the law was to improve educational equity for students from lower-income families by providing federal funds to school districts serving poor students. ESEA was the advent of the source of federal spending on elementary and secondary education. In return for these funds, states and districts were mandated to demonstrate that they are working to meet the needs and providing a quality education to all of their students. The ESEA introduced the notion of broad *accountability*.

The resulting expectations focused on improving schools, and contributed to the complexity of the role of superintendents. Effective superintendents implemented reforms, advised their boards, interfaced with the public, and became adept political strategists. Yet definitions of the role of superintendent varied dramatically among school districts.

The complexity of the superintendent's role necessitates a complex set of areas of expertise as well as the possession of specific skills. No one individual can possess every expertise and skill. In fact, boards of education may have fluctuating demands for superintendents with particular expertise and skills for particular reasons at particular times, depending on the context and needs of the particular school district (Fusarelli, Cooper, and Carella, 2002). Superintendents must interpret their respective board of education's view of the superintendent's role and corresponding demand for expertise, skills, and performance (Finnan et al., 2015).

The evolution of the superintendent position continued into the twenty-first century. The reauthorization of ESEA, the No Child Left Behind Act (NCLB), in the early 2000s highlighted the instructional leadership role inherent in superintendents' responsibilities. NCLB placed stringent performance requirements and benchmarks upon school districts (Björk, Kowalski, and Young, 2005; NCLB, 2001). Though not explicitly stated, the superintendent, as the school district leader, has the ultimate responsibility for school district operations, including NCLB performance standards (Johnstone, Dikkers, and Luedeke, 2009). Thus, NCLB impacted the superintendent in the role areas of instructional program, personnel administration, and stakeholder engagement.

The second significant accountability and reform effort of this century was a 2010 federal grant program called Race to the Top (RTTT). RTTT established a direct link between accountability and evaluations by incentivizing evaluations of individual educators, including school-level leaders, on the basis of student progress (Jacques, Clifford, and Hornung, 2012).

RTTT's focus on student progress meant that the link to educational leader evaluation was to the school-level leader, the principal (Canole and Young, 2013; Jacques, Clifford, and Hornung, 2012). Still, there was no recognition of the district-level leader, the superintendent, and accountability for student progress (Holliday, 2013; Learning Forward, 2017). Thus, despite RTTT's impact on the superintendent in the role area of personnel administration (with a direct link to the instructional program), RTTT maintained a school-based focus.

As standards-based systemic reform started to place increased accountability demands on schools, autonomy over instruction began to shift from individual schools to the school system or school district level (Cohen, Spillane, and Peurach, 2018). Naturally, that shift led to a corresponding shift in responsibility for meeting the accountability demands from the principal to the superintendent.

The third, and most recent, significant reform effort is yet another reauthorization of ESEA, the Every Student Succeeds Act (ESSA) of 2015, which focused on the academic progress of students—the core mission of schools and the primary responsibility of all school leaders. ESSA's flexibility was specifically directed to the state level and district level, not only the school level, a departure from the focus of earlier legislative enactments, including performance evaluation (Herman, Gates, Chavez-Herrerias, and Harris, 2016; Young, Winn, and Reedy, 2017).

ESSA has marked a clear focus on district-level accountability initiatives (Whitehouse, 2017). Thus, ESSA has impacted the superintendent in every role area while also shifting the focus from the school-based focus to the district-based focus for accountability of performance.

Certainly, at the district level, the reform measures of the past two decades have forced an increased focus on the superintendent's role in instructional leadership, curriculum development, and assessment (Bredeson and Kose, 2007). This focus has also challenged superintendents to balance heightened legal and political external demands.

These heightened expectations have not been clearly incorporated into evaluation performance standards for superintendents (Bredeson and Kose, 2007). Superintendent performance expectation criteria and evaluation policy has certainly lagged behind the accountability movement (Mayo and McCartney, 2004).

WHAT ARE THE CRITICAL LEADERSHIP SKILLS
FOR AN EFFECTIVE SUPERINTENDENT?

Although the role of the superintendent is broadly defined, there is agreement that the superintendent is the leader of a school district. "The increasingly complex environment in which public schools are embedded is radically changing the work of school administrators and how they lead" (Hoyle, Bjork, Collier, and Glass, 2005). Warren Bennis (1994) once asserted that more has been written and yet less is known about leadership than any other topic in the social sciences. The designation as "district leader," therefore, adds little clarity to the role.

In seminal writing on organizations across all disciplines, Katz (1955) argued that effective administrators possess basic skill sets. They include:

- Technical skills—specialized knowledge, tools, and techniques
- Conceptual skills—ability to see the big picture
- Human skills—working with people and ethical dimensions

A task force charged with the responsibility of promoting high-quality research in educational leadership (Leithwood and Riehl, 2003) summarized several research-based conclusions about successful leadership:

- Leadership has significant effects on student progress, second only to the effects of quality curriculum and teachers' instruction.
- A core set of leadership practices (setting directions, developing people, and developing the organization) form the "basics" of successful leadership.
- Successful school leaders respond proactively to challenges and opportunities created by the accountability-oriented policy context in which they work.
- Successful school leaders respond productively to the opportunities and challenges of educating diverse groups of students (pp. 2–6).

Note that their research-based conclusions of successful leadership overwhelmingly focus on Human Skills—working with people, building relationships, and behaving ethically to create a shared sense of purpose and direction. The second most important area is Conceptual Skills. School district leaders must be able to "see the big picture" in order to provide a vision and plan for the future. They establish conditions that enable others to be effective in serving students. These skill areas certainly encompass the broad spectrum of superintendent role definitions and provide insight into the critical skills of effective superintendent leaders.

In 2006, Waters and Marzano conducted a meta-analysis to investigate the impact of superintendent leadership on student progress. They examined the findings of twenty-seven studies that involved 2,817 districts and the achievement test scores of 3.4 million students—the largest ever quantitative examination of research on superintendents to date.

Waters and Marzano outlined four major findings:

- District-level leadership matters—they found a statistically significant relationship between district leadership and student progress (using achievement test scores as a measure of progress).

- Effective superintendents focus their efforts on creating goal-oriented districts—leadership responsibilities that have a statistically significant correlation with student progress (using achievement test scores as a measure of progress) relate to setting and keeping districts focused on teaching and learning goals.
- Superintendent tenure is positively correlated with student progress (using achievement test scores as a measure of progress).
- Effective superintendents set clear, nonnegotiable goals for learning and instruction, yet provide school leadership teams with the responsibility and authority for determining how to meet those goals (pp. 3–4).

These findings highlight the importance of quality school district leadership. The authors concluded

> School board members need to hire a superintendent who skillfully fulfills key leadership responsibilities. They need to support district goals for achievement and instruction. They need to support district- and school-level leadership in ways that enhance, rather than diminish, stability. When focused on effective classroom, school, and district practices, appropriate achievement and instructional goals, and effective leadership responsibilities, it is clear that school district leadership matters. (Waters and Marzano, 2006, p. 21)

Despite the research that identifies one particular set of skills as more valuable or effective than others, the practical reality is that superintendents need to interpret their respective board of education's view of the superintendent's role and corresponding demand for expertise, skills, and performance (Finnan et al., 2015). The challenge is that board of education views do not become more narrowly tailored with the focused expectations of accountability and reform efforts. Instead, superintendents are expected to continue to perform to high standards and expectations in every role and facet of their position.

In the AASA's 2010 Decennial Study of the American Superintendent survey and the mid-decade update, every single role and function of the superintendent, except for the superintendent as an applied scientist, was considered very important to the majority of boards of education (Finnan et al., 2015). Expanding expectations, each with associated skills that boards of education rate with high level of importance, are translated into specific superintendent tasks to be evaluated (Glasman and Fuller, 2002). The list of tasks is exponentially growing and serving to make superintendent evaluation extremely complex as years go by.

WHAT IS THE HISTORY OF
SUPERINTENDENT EVALUATION?

In 1980, an attempt was made to clarify the role of superintendent. Representatives of the AASA and National School Boards Association (NSBA) met to define the roles and responsibilities of the superintendent. The joint committee's work generated a publication, *Evaluating the Superintendent* (AASA, 1980), that placed more emphasis on the process of conducting an evaluation than the content of evaluation.

Their meeting also produced a "Joint AASA/NSBA Statement on Superintendent Evaluation" that commented on the prevailing practice of superintendent evaluation and recommended a new process to evaluate superintendents:

> Though individual school board members have many opportunities to observe and evaluate superintendents' performance, it is clear that such informal evaluations cannot provide the board with a complete picture of superintendents' effectiveness in carrying out her (his) complex job. Regular, formal evaluations offer boards the best means of assessing their chief administrator's total performance. Conducted properly they benefit the instructional program of the school district. (AASA, 1980, p. 4)

However, the attention paid to systemically developing and implementing a performance-based evaluation system for superintendents since that time has been uneven at best.

Another event that had a dramatic impact on the role of superintendents was the publication in 1983 of *A Nation at Risk*. This report from the National Commission on Excellence in Education (1983) categorized America's public schools as mediocre and contended that they had placed the future of the nation in jeopardy. The report's major recommendations included:

- Establishing a core curriculum
- Raising academic standards
- Increasing instructional time
- Improving teacher quality
- Recruiting and employing more capable teachers

The report spawned a plethora of other studies and reports that focused on how to improve American public schools. Politicians were quick to jump on the bandwagon and legislate "fixes" for the public schools. The resulting wave of national and state reforms, including the establishment of standards and accountability measures, placed the public's eye on the quality issue once more. This time, however, the focus was on improving student progress. The resulting impact on the expectations and roles of all school professionals, including superintendents, was dramatic.

In an attempt to define the profession of the superintendency, AASA established a commission (1992) that developed a set of eight professional standards and a corresponding set of competencies (textbox 2.1). It was an attempt to stabilize a profession that was confronted by multiple constituencies with different, and often competing, expectations, priorities, and agendas.

The AASA and NSBA convened a joint committee again in 1994 to review the changing environment and resulting modifications in roles and relationships. They identified various "Superintendent Responsibilities" that we categorized under their corresponding AASA Professional Standards (textbox 2.1). Note that the 1992 committee focused on personal competencies required to meet the standards (see textbox 2.1) while the 1994 committee targeted the professional responsibilities superintendents have under each standard (see textbox 2.2).

Textbox 2.1. AASA Professional Standards and Related Competencies

---

AASA Professional Standards and Corresponding Competencies (1992)

Leadership and District Culture
- Demonstrate an awareness of international issues affecting schools and students.
- Maintain personal, physical, and emotional wellness.
- Promote and model risk taking.
- Facilitate comparative planning between constituencies.
- Promote the value of understanding and celebrating school/community cultures.

Policy and Governance
- Describe the system of public school governance in our democracy.
- Relate local policy to state and federal regulations and requirements.
- Describe procedures to avoid civil and criminal liabilities.

Communications and Community Relations
- Demonstrate an understanding of political theory and skills needed to build community support for district priorities.
- Demonstrate that good judgment and actions communicate as well as words.
- Develop formal and informal techniques to gain external perceptions of district by means of surveys, advisory groups, and personal contact.
- Communicate and project an articulate position for education. Write clearly and forcefully.
- Demonstrate formal and informal listening skills. Identify political forces in a community.
- Identify the political context of the community environment. Formulate strategies for passing referenda.
- Identify, track, and deal with issues.

Organizational Management
- Define the major components of quality management.
- Discuss legal concepts, regulations, and codes for school operations.
- Describe the process of delegating responsibility for decision making.
- Use technological applications to enhance administration of business and support systems.
- Demonstrate planning and scheduling of personal time and organization.

Curriculum Planning and Development
- Develop core curriculum design and delivery systems for diverse school communities.
- Describe curriculum planning/future methods to anticipate occupational trends and their educational implications for lifelong learners.
- Demonstrate an understanding of instructional taxonomies, goal objectives, and processes.
- Describe cognitive development and learning theories and their importance to the sequencing of instruction.
- Demonstrate an understanding of child and adolescent growth and development.
- Describe a process to create developmentally appropriate curriculum and instructional practices for all children and adolescents.
- Demonstrate the use of computers and other technologies in educational programming.
- Conduct assessments of present and future student needs.
- Develop a process for faculty input in continued and systematic renewal to ensure appropriate scope, sequence, and content.
- Demonstrate an understanding of curricular alignment to ensure improved student progress and higher-order thinking.

Instructional Management
- Demonstrate an understanding of motivation in the instructional process. Describe classroom management theories and techniques.
- Demonstrate an understanding of the development and progress of the whole student including the physical, social, emotional, cognitive, and linguistic needs.
- Describe instructional strategies that include multicultural sensitivity and diverse learning styles.
- Exhibit applications of computer technology connected to instruction programs. Describe how to interpret and use testing/assessment results to improve education. Demonstrate knowledge of research findings on the use of a variety of instructional strategies.

Human Resources Management
- Demonstrate knowledge of adult learning theory and motivation. Diagnose and improve organizational health and morale.
- Demonstrate personnel management strategies. Understand alternative benefit packages.

continued

- Assess individual and institutional sources of stress and develop methods for reducing stress (e.g., counseling, exercise programs, and diet).
- Demonstrate knowledge of pupil personnel service and categorical programs.

Values and Ethics of Leadership
- Describe the role of schooling in a democratic society.
- Describe a strategy to promote the value that moral and ethical practices are established and practiced in each classroom and school.
- Describe a strategy to ensure that diversity of religion, ethnicity, and way of life in the district are respected.
- Formulate a plan to coordinate social, health, and community agencies to support each child in the district.

Textbox 2.2.   AASA Professional Standards and AASA/NSBA Superintendent Responsibilities

AASA/NSBA Professional Responsibilities (1994)

Leadership and District Culture
- To serve as the school board's chief executive officer and preeminent educational adviser in all efforts of the board to fulfill its school system governance role.
- To propose and institute a process for long-range strategic planning that will engage the board and the community in positioning the school district for success in ensuing years. To develop a description for the board of what constitutes leadership and management of public schools, taking into account that effective leadership and management are the results of effective governance and effective administration combined.
- To collaborate with other administrators through national and state professional associations to inform state legislators, members of Congress, and all other appropriate state and federal officials of local concerns and issues.

Policy and Governance
- To serve as a catalyst for the school system's administrative leadership team in proposing and implementing policy changes.
- To present policy options along with specific recommendations to the board when circumstances require the board to adopt new policies or review existing policies.
- To develop and inform the board of administrative procedures needed to implement board policy.

Communications and Community Relations
- To keep all board members informed about school operations and programs. To interpret the needs of the school system to the board.
- To develop a sound program of school/community relations in concert with the board.

- To develop and carry out a plan for keeping the professional and support staff informed about the mission, goals, and strategies of the school system and about important roles all staff members play in realizing them.
- To provide all board members with complete background information and a recommendation for school board action on each agenda item well in advance of each board meeting.
- To develop and implement a continuing plan for working with the news media.

Organizational Management
- To serve as the primary educational leader for the school system and chief administrative officer of the entire school district's professional and support staff, including staff members assigned to provide support service to the board.
- To oversee management of the district's day-to-day operations.

Curriculum Planning and Development
- None

Instructional Management
- None

Human Resources Management
- To ensure that professional development opportunities are available to all school system employees.
- To evaluate personnel performance in harmony with district policy and to keep the board informed about such evaluations.

Values and Ethics of Leadership
- To ensure that the school system provides equal opportunity for all students.

It is interesting to note that in 1994, when the joint committee defined the eighteen superintendent responsibilities, the responsibilities reflected neither Curriculum Planning and Development nor Instructional Management, two of the eight professional standards directly addressing instructional leadership. The potential impact of high-stakes testing had not yet substantially affected the performance evaluations of superintendents.

This lack of focus on instruction and increased academic performance was evidenced by the criteria commonly used by school boards to evaluate superintendent performance as reported by Glass (1992). The top five, in rank order, were:

- General effectiveness
- Board/superintendent relations
- Management functions
- Budget development and implementation
- Educational leadership/knowledge

Expectations and Performance Assessment: The Disconnect

Comprehensive studies of the superintendency in the 1990s (Glass, 1992; Robinson and Bickers, 1990; Stufflebeam, 1995) revealed some disturbing patterns in the process of superintendent evaluation. Although about 90 percent of superintendents nationally were evaluated annually, less than 10 percent of the superintendents said that their board discussed explicit guidelines and performance standards with them when they were hired. The various researchers also found that superintendents were not really evaluated against criteria in their job descriptions.

Additionally, these studies confirmed that evaluations leading to termination were too often grounded in personality and board relationship issues. Hoyle and Skrla (1999) contended that a superintendent may receive the highest ratings on most of the evaluation criteria but be nonrenewed due to personality conflicts and politics that are beyond the superintendent's control. Two evaluative criteria stood out in these studies as most important in practice: board/superintendent relationships and general effectiveness of performance.

Even more telling were the two criteria identified as having "little or no" importance in evaluative process: student progress outcomes and student/superintendent relationships. By the middle of the 1990s high-stakes tests were established in many states. The constant comparison of schools and school districts by their students' scores on state tests as the measure of student progress put school system leaders in the "fish bowl" of accountability.

The expectations and role of the superintendent quickly evolved in the direction of improving student progress. Local boards and board members across the nation "heard" the public concern and by 2000, the NSBA proclaimed that the "key work" of school boards was improving student progress (Gemberling, Smith, and Villani, 2000, p. 1). As we will discuss further in chapter 4, a proclamation about the role of the board of education and superintendent performance expectations related to student progress have farther reaching implications that must be considered beyond mere words of proclamation.

In this twenty-first century, effective superintendents must possess instructional, political, and managerial expertise to successfully lead school districts. More than ever, they must be instructional leaders, whose responsibilities reach into the heart of classrooms—student progress. This new role is reflected by the top four expectations school boards have of superintendents. They are, in rank order:

- Educational leader
- Political leader
- Managerial leader
- Leader of reform (Glass, Bjork, and Brunner, 2000)

A comparison of evaluation criteria most commonly used up to the early 1990s with these expectations, in rank order, reveal the changing expectations of the performance of superintendents that boards use to evaluate their performance (table 2.1).

Table 2.1. Comparison of Evaluation Criteria 1992 and Board Expectations 2000

1992	2000
General effectiveness	Educational leader
Board/superintendent relations	Political leader
Management functions	Managerial leader
Budget development and implementation	Leader of reform

Sources: Glass, 1992; Glass, Bjork, and Bruner, 2000.

Evaluations should be based in the generic duties of particular professional groups (Scriven, 1994). Determining job expectations is a logical and necessary initial step in designing a superintendent evaluation system. Doing so bases performance assessment on the professional competencies and duties of the position (Candoli, Cullen, and Stufflebeam, 1997).

Superintendents are the chief executive officers of school districts: "Executives, by definition, are considered to be responsible for organizational outcomes whether or not they exercise direct influence over the achievement of outcomes" (Duke, 1992, p. 114). Although there is increasing consensus that assessments of student progress must be used in educational evaluation (Candoli et al., 1997), student progress alone does not capture the realm of public expectations, nor does it capture the day-to-day realities of the responsibilities of school superintendents.

WHAT ARE THE PURPOSES OF SUPERINTENDENT EVALUATION?

Superintendents often quip that board members are only willing to devote the time required to perform a formal evaluation when they are not satisfied with their superintendent's performance and are attempting to terminate their superintendent's employment. Superintendents are the only school system employees not supervised or evaluated by another licensed professional. Yet superintendents must be evaluated.

As we will discuss in chapter 3, many states have adopted legislation requiring boards to regularly evaluate their superintendents. Besides fulfilling a legal requirement, the process can be a valuable tool and serve a broad range of purposes, such as:

- Defining the board's expectations of the superintendent
- Enhancing superintendent/board communications
- Identifying and prioritizing school system goals
- Clarifying the roles of the board and superintendent
- Improving board/superintendent relations
- Enhancing the planning process
- Improving educational performance
- Making personnel decisions
- Holding the superintendent accountable

Superintendents want and need feedback from their boards. It is difficult to grow professionally without it. Evaluations provide superintendents an opportunity to assess their board's satisfaction with their performance. The evaluation process also gives board members an opportunity to assess the superintendent's satisfaction with the board's performance and the job itself.

Models of Performance Assessment

In an effort to improve the evaluation of superintendents in America's school systems, the Center for Research on Educational Accountability and Teacher Evaluation (CREATE) completed a research project to provide "the foundation for future development of improved models for evaluating school district superintendents" (Candoli et al., 1997, p. 7). They described and assessed current evaluation models and provided a draft of an "improved" model that attempts to consider multifaceted superintendent performance in evaluating overall performance.

The study by CREATE identified twelve distinct models of superintendent evaluation. In their report, the models were categorized by the three general methods used to draw conclusions from the evaluation process: (1) global judgment, (2) judgment driven by criteria, and (3) judgment driven by data.

- Global judgment consisted of several prominent evaluation practices, including school board judgment, descriptive narrative reports, and/or formative exchanges about performance.
- Judgment Driven by Criteria consisted of printed rating forms, report cards, management by objectives (MBO), performance contracting, and/or duties-based evaluation. This category is comparable to results-focused appraisals of business models.
- Judgment Driven by Data was also related to the results-focused appraisals of business models and includes superintendent portfolios, student progress outcome measures, and school and district accreditation.

Table 2.2 depicts the twelve models as they were categorized.

Table 2.2.   Superintendent Evaluation Models

Global Judgment	Judgment Driven by Specified Criteria	Judgment Driven by Data
Board Judgment	Printed Rating Forms	Superintendent Portfolio
Descriptive Narrative Reports	Report Cards	Student Progress Outcome Measures
Formative Exchanges about Performance	Management by Objectives	School and District
Stakeholder Evaluation	Performance Contracting Duties-Based Evaluation	Accreditation

CREATE researchers evaluated each of the identified models using the personnel evaluation standards established by the Joint Committee on Standards for Educational Evaluation (JCSEE) (2009). All of the models evaluated contained relative strengths and weaknesses. However, those that have the greatest potential to meet the essential criteria for quality personnel evaluation (Candoli et al., 1997; JCSEE, 2009) include:

- Duties-based evaluation
- Superintendent portfolios
- The use of student progress outcome measures

Including these features in superintendent evaluation would enable boards to enjoy the benefits of the strengths of each model while compensating for individual models' weaknesses.

Board members are most often lay people with a primary orientation to and knowledge of assessment models used in the private sector. A comparison of the Candoli, Cullen, and Stufflebeam superintendent evaluation models with business evaluation models (Grote, 1996) reveals considerable overlap between the two worlds, as presented in figure 2.1.

The comparison of the models from the two sectors indicated:

- Global Judgment is closely related to the global appraisals proposed by Grote (1996) in describing business models. They represent the simplest of appraisals and rely on the raters' knowledge of the overall performance of the superintendent and require well-trained appraisers.
- Judgment Driven by Criteria corresponds and overlaps with both results-focused and behaviorally anchored business models. Rating scales,

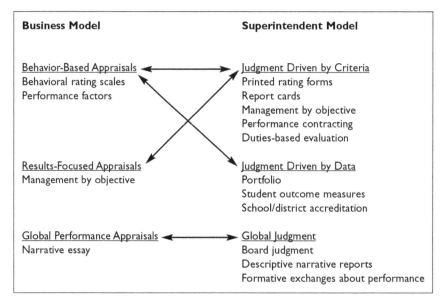

Figure 2.1.   Comparison of Business Appraisal and Superintendent Evaluation Models

specified performance factors, outcome measures, and objectives drive these appraisals.

- Judgment Driven by Data is closely related to the behaviorally anchored business model. This model is duties based with a focus on performance and outcome measures.

SUMMARY

The hue and cry for accountability at all levels demands the fair evaluation of all personnel, including the superintendent. We suggest that a fair evaluation of the superintendent requires greater congruence among:

- District goals
- Evaluation instruments
- Actual duties performed by superintendents
- Standards that guide the profession

At the same time, the evaluation models and evidence of achievement must be well suited to meet all the standards for quality personnel evaluation.

REFERENCES

American Association of School Administrators. (1980). *Evaluating the superintendent.* Arlington, VA: Author.

American Association of School Administrators. (1992). *Professional standards for the superintendency.* Arlington, VA: Author.

Bennis, W. (1994). *On becoming a leader.* Reading, MA: Addison-Wesley.

Björk, L. G., Kowalski, T. J., and Young, M. D. (2005). National education reform reports. In L. G. Björk and T. J. Kowalski (Eds.), *The contemporary superintendent: Preparation, practice, and development* (pp. 45–69). Thousand Oaks, CA: Corwin Press.

Bredeson, P. V., and Kose, B. W. (2007). Responding to the education reform agenda: A study of school superintendents' instructional leadership. *Education Policy Analysis Archives*, 15(5), 2–23.

Candoli, I. C., Cullen, K., and Stufflebeam, D. L. (1997). *Superintendent performance evaluation: Current practice and directions for improvement.* Boston: Kluwer Academic Publishers.

Canole, M., and Young, M. (2013). *Standards for educational leaders: An analysis.* Washington, DC: Council of Chief State School Officers.

Carter, G. R., and Cunningham, W. G. (1997). *The American school superintendent: Leading in an age of pressure.* San Francisco, CA: Jossey-Bass.

Cohen, D. K., Spillane, J. P., and Peurach, D. J. (2018). The dilemmas of educational reform. *Educational Researcher*, 47, 204–12. doi:10.3102/0013189X17743488

DiPaola, M. F., and Stronge, J. H. (2001). Superintendent evaluation in a standards-based environment: A status report from the states. *Journal of Personnel Evaluation in Education*, 1.5(2), 97–110.

Duke, D. (1992). Concepts of administrative effectiveness and the evaluation of school administrators. *Journal of Personnel Evaluation in Education*, 6(2), 103–22.

Elementary and Secondary Education Act as amended by the Every Student Succeeds Act, 20 U.S.C. §6301 et seq. (2015).

Finnan, L. A., McCord, R. S., Stream, C. C., Mattocks, T. C., Peterson, G. J., and Ellerson, N. M. (2015). *Study of the American superintendent: 2015 mid-decade update.* Alexandria, VA: American Association of School Administrators.

Fusarelli, L. D., Cooper, B. S., and Carella, V. A. (2002). Dilemmas of the modern superintendency. In B. S. Cooper and L. D. Fusarelli (Eds.), *The promises and perils facing today's school superintendent* (pp. 5–20). Lanham, MD: Scarecrow Press.

Gemberling, K. W., Smith, C. W., and Villani, J. S. (2000). *The keywork of school boards guidebook.* Alexandria, VA: National School Board Association.

Glasman, N. S., and Fuller, J. (2002). Superintendent evaluation: Concepts, practices, and an outcome-related case. In B. S. Cooper and L. D. Fusarelli (Eds.), *The promises and perils facing today's school superintendent* (pp. 133–52). Lanham, MD: Scarecrow Press.

Glass, T. E. (1992). *The 1992 study of the American superintendency.* Arlington, VA: American Association of School Administrators.

Glass, T. E., Bjork, L., and Brunner, C. C. (2000). *The study of the American school superintendency: A look at the superintendent of education in the new millennium.* Arlington, VA: American Association of School Administrators.

Grote, D. (1996). *The complete guide to performance appraisal.* New York: American Management Association.

Herman, R., Gates, S. M., Chavez-Herrerias, E. R., and Harris, M. (2016). School leadership interventions under the Every Student Succeeds Act [Research report]. Retrieved from RAND Corporation website: https://www.rand.org/content/dam/rand/pubs/research_reports/RR1500/RR1550/RAND_RR1550.pdf.

Holliday, T. K. (2013). Tying superintendent performance to teachers, principals. *School Administrator,* 70(7), 12–13.

Hoyle, J. R., Bjork, L. G., Collier, V., and Glass, T. (2005). *The superintendent as CEO: Standards-based performance.* Thousand Oaks, CA: Corwin Press.

Hoyle, J. R., and Skrla, L. (1999). The politics of superintendent evaluation. *Journal of Personnel Evaluation in Education,* 13(4), 405–19.

Jacques, C., Clifford, M., and Hornung, K. (2012). *Principal evaluation policy landscape: A survey of state policies.* Washington, DC: Center on Great Teachers and Leaders.

Johnstone, C., Dikkers, A. G., and Luedeke, A. (2009). Educational leadership in the era of accountability. *Educational Considerations,* 36(2), 14–18.

Joint Committee on Standards for Educational Evaluation. (1994). *The program evaluation standards.* Newbury, VA: Sage.

Joint Committee on Standards for Educational Evaluation (2009). *The personnel evaluation standards: How to assess systems for evaluating educators.* Thousand Oaks, CA: Corwin Press.

Katz, R. L. (1955). Skills of an effective administrator. *Harvard Business Review,* 33(1), 33–42.

Learning Forward. (2017). A new vision for professional learning: A toolkit to help states advance learning and improvement systems. Retrieved from https://learningforward.org/docs/default-source/getinvolved/essa/essanewvisiontoolkit.

Leithwood, K. A., and Riehl, C. (2003). *What we know about successful school leadership.* Philadelphia, PA: Laboratory for Student Success, Temple University.

Mayo, C. R., and McCartney, G. P. (2004). School superintendents' evaluations: Effective and results-based? *ERS Spectrum,* 22(1), 19–33.

National Commission on Excellence in Education. (1983). *A nation at risk: The imperative for educational reform.* Washington, DC: U.S. Government Printing Office.

No Child Left Behind (NCLB) Act of 2001, 20 U.S.C.A. § 6301 et seq.

Potter, R. E. (1967). *The stream of American education.* New York: American Book Company.

Robinson, G., and Bickers, P. (1990). *Evaluation of superintendents and school boards.* Arlington, VA: Educational Research Service.

Scriven, M. (1994). Duties of the teacher. *Journal of Personnel Evaluation in Education,* 8(2), 151–84.

Stronge, J. H. (Ed.). (1997). *Evaluating teaching: A guide to current thinking and best practice.* Thousand Oaks, CA: Corwin Press.

Stuart v. School District No. 1 of Village of Kalamazoo, 1874.

Stufflebeam, D. L. (1995). Evaluation of superintendent performance: Toward a general model. In A. McConney (Ed.), *Studies in educational evaluation*, 21(2), 153–225. New York, NY: Elsevier.

Waters, J. T., and Marzano, R. J. (2006). School district leadership that works: The effect of superintendent leadership on student achievement (Report No. ED494270). Retrieved from http://www.eric.ed.gov.

Whitehouse, E. (2017, July/August). What the Every Student Succeeds Act means for state education leaders. The Current State [e-newsletter of The Council of State Governments]. Retrieved from http://www.csg.org/pubs/capitolideas/enews/cs46_1.aspx.

Young, M. D., Winn, K. M., and Reedy, M. A. (2017). The Every Student Succeeds Act: Strengthening the focus on educational leadership. *Educational Administration Quarterly*, 53, 705–26. doi:10.1177/0013161X17735871.

Chapter Three

Current Status of Superintendent Evaluation State by State

*Chapter adapted from Schneider, T. L. (2019). A state-level superintendent evaluation policy analysis (Doctoral dissertation). Retrieved from ProQuest Dissertations and Theses (10977630).

Superintendent evaluations can and should serve as a key tool to improve educational performance (Marzano and Waters, 2009). To do so, superintendent evaluations must be held to the same standard of quality assurance as any other evaluation.

Yet the unique structure and political nature of the superintendent evaluation process coupled with the changing role of the superintendent in the shadows of the accountability and reform movement make superintendent evaluation more challenging than evaluations of other school personnel. The challenge often leads to avoidance, an unwillingness to ask the hard questions, and measure the quality of current superintendent evaluation process structures, or to an evaluation that fails to meet the basic minimal criteria for fair and accurate evaluation.

In 2000, the authors of the first edition of this book completed a national study of the fifty states to assess current policies and practices in superintendent evaluation to determine the extent to which performance criteria in practice were compatible with the professional standards. Since the early 2000's state-level superintendent evaluation policies have not received significant research attention, have not been investigated in the context of the influential accountability movement (Mayo and McCartney, 2004), and have not undergone a systematic state-by-state status review. Consequently, we recently completed a national review of state-level superintendent evaluation policies to update the current status of this critical process.

In this chapter, we will provide a current picture of the quality of superintendent evaluation policies at the state level. In particular, we will address the following questions:

1. Why does superintendent evaluation policy need to be addressed at the state level?
2. What makes a quality superintendent evaluation policy at the state level?
3. What is the current status of existing state policies that govern superintendent evaluation?
4. What does the current status of superintendent evaluation policy at the state level mean for practice?

WHY DOES SUPERINTENDENT EVALUATION POLICY NEED TO BE ADDRESSED AT THE STATE LEVEL?

In previous chapters we shared the importance of ensuring that any superintendent evaluation process be conceptually sound. Conceptual soundness of the evaluation begins at the state level. Though the federal government has weighed-in more heavily on education policy matters over the past two decades, education policy is still largely within the purview and control of the states (Fowler, 2013; Kraft and Furlong, 2018). Even when the federal government weighs in, as it has with accountability and school reform, such efforts do not become systemic until states enact the reforms with detailed policy (Parker, 1995).

The current federal accountability and reform legislation, the Every Student Succeeds Act (ESSA), intentionally declines to dictate that states adopt a particular teacher or educational leader evaluation system. This absence of any federal mandate leaves the responsibility for educational leader evaluation systems, and more specifically, superintendent evaluation systems, squarely at the state level, or local level (Elementary and Secondary Education Act as amended by the Every Student Succeeds Act [ESSA], 2015), where states have delegated that control and conditioned local capacity to act (Björk, Browne-Ferrigno, and Kowalski, 2014). Thus, while superintendent evaluation may seem localized, it is or can be governed at the state level for consistency and coherence (DiPaola and Stronge, 2001a) and to serve as the connecting link between federal accountability initiatives and localized action.

Moreover, the accountability and reform movement, specifically with the passage of ESSA, has begun to shift responsibility for school outcomes from the individual school level to the school district level (Cohen, Spillane, and Peurach, 2018; ESSA, 2015). ESSA removed the focus from student- or school-based requirements, instead focusing on state plans for district or system-based requirements like hiring, professional learning, and evaluation (ESSA, 2015; Learning Forward, 2017).

ESSA's shift in responsibility for outcomes highlighted the need for a corresponding shift in performance expectations from the school level to the district level, with oversight at the state level. "While the transformation of an accountability system represents an enormously important step toward improved system performance, the process remains incomplete unless leadership evaluation becomes as multifaceted and constructive as the best accountability systems" (Reeves, 2008, p. 13).

Without such a state-level analysis, increased local control can have a significant impact on superintendent evaluation policies because of their unique structure and presence in a politically influenced environment. Longevity in the position of superintendent is directly related to the superintendent's ability to understand the board of education's political and power structures (Boyd, 1976; Keedy and Björk, 2002) and to maintain a strong relationship with the board of education that can rise above the politics.

In the most recent study of American superintendents (Finnan et al., 2015), superintendents reported that their performance was most inhibited by politics. If a superintendent does not respond or adjust to board of education expectations, even those that are politically motivated, the superintendent's tenure is likely to be cut short. Whereas, if states retain a strong voice in superintendent evaluation policies, limiting autonomy of the local board of education, superintendents may not need to adjust to sometimes politically motivated local evaluation expectations. State-level superintendent evaluation policy can help to ensure that a fair, equitable, and high-quality process is in place to protect the superintendent and board relationship and to buffer the political game playing.

Ultimately, well-formed state-level superintendent evaluation policies provide the structure that supports the board of education and superintendent relationship, ensures fair and high-quality superintendent performance evaluation, protects against "political game playing" (Hoyle and Skrla, 1999, p. 405), and improves the district's ability to grow and, if necessary, reform (Henrikson, 2018). A structured performance evaluation can potentially provide district-wide benefits of improved communication, budgeting, planning, accountability, and overall school improvement and reform (DiPaola and Stronge, 2001a, 2001b, 2003; Mayo and McCartney, 2004).

Conversely, poorly formed or nonexistent state-level superintendent evaluation policies can lead to unqualified, often uninformed, local control. In turn, unqualified, uninformed local control can lead to the breakdown of the board of education and superintendent relationship, the invasion of "political game playing" (Hoyle and Skrla, 1999, p. 405), rapid superintendent turnover, and the deterioration of goals and policies necessary for school reform (Alsbury, 2008; Grady and Bryant, 1989).

WHAT MAKES A QUALITY SUPERINTENDENT EVALUATION POLICY AT THE STATE LEVEL?

Conceptual soundness of superintendent evaluation at the state level requires measuring coherence of superintendent evaluation policy provisions with the four criteria established by the Joint Committee on Standards for Educational Evaluation (JCSEE) (1988, 2009). We introduced the JCSEE criteria in chapter 1 as standards of quality for all personnel evaluation systems. Recall that the JCSEE criteria standards include propriety, utility, feasibility, and accuracy.

For the purposes of providing a picture of the current status of state-level superintendent evaluation policies, those standards were translated into components and indicators that measured a state policy's coherence with the JCSEE quality standards. The component and indicators not only reflected the intention of the JCSEE as outlined in table 1.1 but also recognized the unique intricacies and political nature of the superintendent evaluation process and the historical changing role of the superintendent in light of the federal accountability movement as we discussed in chapter 2.

The components and indicators were developed, in part, using DiPaola's (2010) work to translate the JCSEE standards into superintendent evaluation criteria components and using the Databases on State Teacher and Principal Evaluation Policies (American Institutes for Research, 2018) and used for principal evaluation policy (Jacques, Clifford, and Hornung, 2012). The latter were modified to reflect appropriate distinctions between principal and superintendent role and performance expectations.

The resulting rubric of standards, components, and indicators is set forth in tables 3.1–3.4.

Using the rubric, a content analysis was performed on state-level superintendent evaluation policies. For the purpose of this study, state-level superintendent evaluation policy was defined as state statutes, state board of education regulations, and state board of education guidance documents mandating the existence and content of superintendent evaluations, for each of the fifty states and Washington, DC.

We recognize national and state school governance associations, including the American Association of School Administrators (AASA) and the National School Boards Association (NSBA), along with respective state-

Table 3.1.   State-Level Superintendent Evaluation Policy Criteria Propriety Standard

CRITERIA STANDARD	CRITERIA CATEGORY	CRITERIA INDICATOR
(Joint Committee, 1988, 2009)	*(DiPaola, 2010; Jacques, Clifford, & Hornung, 2012)*	*(American Institutes for Research, 2018; Jacques, Clifford, & Hornung, 2012)*
Propriety Standards	**Data Collection Procedures: Evaluators**	Does the state mandate exclusion of evaluators who may have a conflict of interest within the superintendent evaluation process?
		Does the state mandate training for evaluators in conducting the superintendent evaluation?
		Does the state mandate any additional oversight to ensure evaluators implement the superintendent evaluation system with fidelity?
	Data Collection Procedures: Stakeholder Involvement & Communication	Does the state require or permit involvement of professional educational associations in development of the superintendent evaluation policy?
		If so, which professional educational associations are involved (e.g., national or administrator associations; national or state school boards associations)? ***Note: this question is not scored but is included for descriptive analysis purposes only.***
		If so, what roles do professional educational associations play, advisory or authoritative? ***Note: this question is not scored but is included for descriptive analysis purposes only.***
		Does the state require or permit non-board member stakeholder participation in the superintendent evaluation?
	Methods for Using Results	Does the state mandate confidentiality of the superintendent evaluation?

Table 3.2. State-Level Superintendent Evaluation Policy Criteria Utility Standard

CRITERIA STANDARD (Joint Committee, 1988, 2009)	CRITERIA CATEGORY (DiPaola, 2010; Jacques, Clifford, & Hornung, 2012)	CRITERIA INDICATOR (American Institutes for Research, 2018; Jacques, Clifford, & Hornung, 2012)
Utility Standards	Evaluation Goals & Purposes	Does the state identify a goal or purpose for superintendent evaluation?
		If so, what does the state identify as its goal or purpose for superintendent evaluation (e.g., accountability, Every Student Succeeds Act, coherence with preparation and licensure, coherence with locally developed goals and purposes)? *Note: this question is not scored but is included for descriptive analysis purposes only.*
	Data Collection Procedures: Selected Performance Criteria and Measures	Does the state mandate particular superintendent evaluation criteria or components?
		Do the mandated criteria or components directly name any existing professional educational standards or reflect at least 75% of any existing professional educational standards even if such standards are not directly named?
		If so, which professional educational standards are specifically referenced (e.g., AASA, NSBA, PSEL, state-developed standards)? *Note: this question is not scored but is included for descriptive analysis purposes only.*
		Does the state identify evaluation components that specifically reference the goals or purpose for superintendent evaluation?
		Does the state mandate inclusion of student progress measures in the superintendent evaluation?
	Methods for Using Results	Does the state mandate or permit superintendent contractual provisions based upon evaluation results?
		Does the state mandate or permit evaluation results to be used for development of a professional growth plan (or similar document) or other human resource decisions?

Table 3.3. State-Level Superintendent Evaluation Policy Criteria Feasibility Standard

CRITERIA STANDARD (Joint Committee, 1988, 2009)	CRITERIA CATEGORY (DiPaola, 2010; Jacques, Clifford, & Hornung, 2012)	CRITERIA INDICATOR (American Institutes for Research, 2018; Jacques, Clifford, & Hornung, 2012)
Feasibility Standards	**Data Collection Procedures: Frequency of Evaluation**	Does the state dictate frequency of superintendent evaluation?
	Data Collection Procedures: Reporting	Does the state maintain a superintendent evaluation process data tracking system?
		Does the state require districts to report superintendent evaluation results to the state?

affiliated or connected associations, have taken an active role in superintendent evaluation forms and procedures (DiPaola and Stronge, 2003). Thus, state-level superintendent evaluation policy was defined as including national or state school governance associations (whether administrator or board) but only when statute, regulation, or state board of education guidance documents explicitly referenced these associations.

WHAT IS THE CURRENT STATUS OF EXISTING STATE POLICIES THAT GOVERN SUPERINTENDENT EVALUATION?

To gain a complete and accurate picture of the current status of existing state policies that govern superintendent evaluation, three questions were asked:

- Does the state have a superintendent evaluation policy?
- If the state has a superintendent evaluation policy, to what extent does the state update the policy with changes to the accountability and reform movement?
- If the state has a superintendent evaluation policy, to what extent does the state policy meet each of the JCSEE standards: propriety, utility, feasibility, and accuracy?

For the remainder of this chapter, we review the findings to provide a picture of the current status of state policies that govern superintendent evaluation and the implications of those findings at the local level.

Table 3.4. State-Level Superintendent Evaluation Policy Criteria Accuracy Standard

CRITERIA STANDARD (Joint Committee, 1988, 2009)	CRITERIA CATEGORY (DiPaola, 2010; Jacques, Clifford, & Hornung, 2012)	CRITERIA INDICATOR (American Institutes for Research, 2018; Jacques, Clifford, & Hornung, 2012)
Accuracy Standards	**Data Collection Procedures: Data Integrity**	Does the state mandate that multiple sources of data must be used in the superintendent evaluation process?
		Does the state assign different weights to different sources of superintendent evaluation data?
		Does the state mandate a particular form for the superintendent evaluation?
		Does the state identify evaluators for the superintendent evaluation?
		Does the state mandate that multiple evaluator sources be used in the superintendent evaluation process?
	Methods for Summarizing Results & System Evaluation	Does the state mandate a process to assess the state-level superintendent evaluation system's effectiveness?
		Did the state pilot the superintendent evaluation system model process or form?
		Does the state identify outcomes to determine overall effectiveness of state-level superintendent evaluation system?
	System Structure: Recognition of District-Specific Demographics	Does the state differentiate between type of district (e.g., rural, urban, suburban) in the superintendent evaluation process?
		Does the state differentiate between any district demographics in the superintendent evaluation process?

Seventeen States Do Not Have Superintendent Evaluation Policies at the State Level

The majority of the states, 67 percent (thirty-four states), had a state-level superintendent evaluation policy. Though a minority, still 34 percent of states (seventeen states) did not have any state-level superintendent evaluation policy. States that did not have a state-level superintendent evaluation policy included Alabama, Alaska, Arkansas, California, Colorado, Florida, Indiana, Louisiana, Maine, Maryland, Minnesota, Nevada, New Mexico, Oregon, South Dakota, Utah, and Vermont. California required evaluation for the chief executive officer in a private school but did not maintain a similar requirement for the superintendent in a public school.

Comparisons were made among the seventeen states that did not have a state-level superintendent evaluation policy to examine inferential explanations for the nonexistence of such policies. In particular, student enrollment was examined with the presumption that much like student enrollment influences the performance expectations and daily responsibilities of the superintendent (Jones and Howley, 2009), lower student enrollment could potentially result in the decision not to have a policy.

A state's superintendent selection structure (i.e., whether the superintendent can be elected or appointed) was also examined on the presumption that elected superintendents can be seen as having their evaluation take place by election, rather than by formal evaluation procedures. Thus, a state with elected superintendents may deem it unnecessary to have a state-level superintendent evaluation policy requirement. Despite this further examination, no clear connections or commonalities were identified within those seventeen states to explain the nonexistence of superintendent evaluation policy.

In addition to states that did not have any superintendent evaluation policy, there were eight states that had a policy, but the policies did not contain a large number of indicators. These states scored three or below on the total rubric score and included North Dakota, Kentucky, New Hampshire, Rhode Island, South Carolina, Washington, DC, Wisconsin, and Arizona. The low number of indicators present in these policies provides little more than a technical legal requirement for the board of education to evaluate the superintendent. These states essentially leave superintendent evaluation policy to local control, some expressly and some by implication.

Finally, in considering whether states mandate superintendent evaluation policy, consideration was provided to a state's use of mandatory or permissive provisions. Delaware and Michigan mandated rather than permitted policy indicators in ratios of 15:2 and 16:2, respectively. By contrast, Missouri and Ohio permitted rather than mandated the indicators in ratios of 13:2 and 11:2, respectively. Ohio even used terminology that designated its superintendent evaluation policy system as a voluntary system. Whether a state selects mandatory or permissive provisions signals its philosophy on superintendent evaluation, its philosophy on local control of education policy, and foreshadows its implementation efforts.

State-Level Superintendent Evaluation Policy Revisions Patterns Suggest Loose Alignment with Passage of Federal Accountability Legislation

A pattern emerged that suggested states adopt or revise superintendent evaluation policy loosely aligned with the federal accountability movement (i.e., the 2001 passage of No Child Left Behind [NCLB], the 2010 federal grant program, Race to the Top [RTTT], and the 2015 passage of the Every Student Succeeds Act [ESSA]). Notably, only five states had any policy language governing superintendent evaluation prior to 2000 and the passage of federal accountability legislation. These states were Arizona, Missouri, New Jersey, Oklahoma, and Rhode Island.

Another nine states adopted policy language in the early to mid-2000s, following the passage of NCLB. These states included Connecticut, Illinois, Iowa, New York, Ohio, South Carolina, Texas, Virginia, and West Virginia. The vast majority of the remaining sixteen states, of the thirty-four states with superintendent evaluation policies, only adopted policy language after 2010. This policy action followed RTTT and the passage of ESSA.

Though no clear evidence of the connection between policy language adoption and federal accountability law adoption was noted, there is at least the presumption of a connection. This presumption exists given the close proximity of time that states may have adopted or revised policy language related to superintendent evaluation policy in response to federal accountability legislation.

State-Level Superintendent Evaluation Policies Demonstrate Mixed Coherence with the JCSEE Standards

One thing is clear, states are not developing or adopting superintendent evaluation policies with the JCSEE standards in mind. Despite the thirty-year existence of the JCSEE standards, only one state, Virginia, explicitly linked the superintendent evaluation policy to these standards. Certainly, coherence is still possible without explicit reference to the JCSEE standards in the policy documents but harder to measure with so much policy variation across each JCSEE standard.

As table 3.5 reflects, of the thirty-four states with policies, the highest rubric score was 18.5 and the lowest rubric score was 1.5 out of twenty-five possible points.

Table 3.5.   State Total Rubric Score Ranking

State	Total Rubric Score	State	Total Rubric Score
Massachusetts	18.50	Georgia	6.50
Michigan	17.00	Nebraska	5.50
Delaware	16.00	Oklahoma	5.50
New Jersey	14.50	Idaho	5.00
Kansas	14.00	New York	4.00
West Virginia	12.50	Pennsylvania	4.00
Hawaii	12.00	Tennessee	4.00
North Carolina	11.50	Connecticut	3.50
Virginia	11.50	Illinois	3.50
Iowa	11.00	North Dakota	3.00
Wyoming	11.00	Kentucky	2.50
Mississippi	10.50	New Hampshire	2.00
Missouri	8.50	Rhode Island	2.00
Montana	8.50	South Carolina	2.00
Ohio	7.50	Washington, D.C.	2.00
Washington	7.00	Wisconsin	2.00
Texas	6.50	Arizona	1.50

Propriety Standard. Overall, states did not exhibit depth of policy on the propriety standard. With six indicators, the maximum total possible propriety standard score by each state was six. None of the states has a policy that contained every propriety standard indicator and, therefore, no states achieved a perfect score of six. Four states were closest to a perfect score. Massachusetts, Michigan, New Jersey, and West Virginia had either mandatory or permissive provisions for every indicator except one.

However, the vast majority were at the other end of the scoring spectrum. Approximately 80 percent (twenty-seven of thirty-four states) of states with policies scored two or less on the propriety standard. In fact, the most frequent score was zero, meaning that most frequently, states did not have superintendent evaluation policies that contained any propriety indicators.

Table 3.6 presents the frequency of rubric scores for each indicator of the propriety standard.

Table 3.6. Statewide Frequency of Rubric Scores by Indicator for the Propriety Standard

Indicator	1	0.5	0
Data Collection Procedures: Evaluators			
Indicator A: Does the state mandate exclusion of evaluators who may have a conflict of interest within the superintendent process?	0	0	34
Indicator B: Does the state mandate training for evaluators in conducting a superintendent evaluation?	9	1	24
Indicator C: Does the state mandate any additional oversight to ensure evaluators implement the superintendent evaluation system with fidelity?	9	1	24
Data Collection Procedures: Stakeholder Involvement & Communication			
Indicator D: Does the state require or permit involvement of professional educational associations in development of the superintendent evaluation policy?	3	7	24
Indicator E: Does the state require or permit non-board member stakeholder participation in the superintendent evaluation?	8	9	17
Methods for Using Results			
Indicator F: Does the state mandate confidentiality or public disclosure of the superintendent evaluation?	13	1	20

Note: Thirty-four state scores are reflected; seventeen states did not have a policy and were not scored.

Five indicators (*Indicators A–E*) are worth noting in the propriety standard:

1. **Exclusion of Evaluators with Conflicts of Interest** (*Indicator A*): There was one indicator that clearly stood out as possible contributors to lower scores. Not a single state had a policy provision that addressed the exclusion of evaluators with conflicts of interest.
2. **Training for Board Member Evaluators** (*Indicator B*): Ten of the thirty-four states with policies had provisions for board member evaluator training. This showed slightly more coherence with the propriety standard.
3. **State Oversight to Ensure System Implementation with Fidelity** (*Indicator C*): Ten states have provisions for state oversight to ensure fidelity in the implementation of the state evaluation system. Of note, one of the states that did maintain oversight in the implementation process, Kansas,

directly tied such oversight to the accountability and reform movement and the state's ESSA plan. However, most oversight came in the form of state review and approval of local superintendent evaluation policy. Kentucky, Michigan, Nebraska, New York, and Texas required some form of policy review and approval. Michigan actually required the local board of education to post the superintendent evaluation policy publicly on the board's website along with the research base that supports the policy development.

4. **Stakeholder Involvement and Communication** (*Indicators D and E*): Ten of the thirty-four states with superintendent evaluation policies provided for the involvement of professional associations in the state superintendent policy development process. The vast majority of professional association involvement included state affiliates or state associations connected with the AASA and the NSBA. Most states, six of the ten states that utilized professional associations, utilized the professional associations in an advisory manner only.

The indicator accounting for the most depth in states meeting the propriety standard was the requirement for non-board member stakeholder participation in the superintendent evaluation process. This included any non-board member participation—that is, participation of the superintendents themselves, participation of staff, participation of students, and/or participation of the community/general public. Half (seventeen) of the thirty-four states with policies had policy provisions that provided for the involvement of non-board member stakeholders. Of those seventeen, nine states made such involvement permissive while eight made such involvement mandatory.

A summary of each state's score on the propriety standard by criteria, category, and indicator is contained in Appendix M.

Utility Standard. Unlike the propriety standard findings, overall, states exhibited more depth of policy on the utility standard. With seven indicators, the maximum total possible utility standard score for each state was seven. Three states—Hawaii, Kansas, and Massachusetts—had a policy that contained every utility standard indicator. These three states met some indicators permissively, and therefore, did not receive a perfect score of seven. An additional eight states—Delaware, Iowa, Mississippi, Missouri, New Jersey, North Carolina, Ohio, and Virginia—had policies that contained either permissive or mandatory provisions for six of the seven indicators.

States received the widest range of scores on the utility standard. There was no clear majority of scores. Like the propriety standard, of states with superintendent evaluation policies, the most frequent score was zero, meaning that most frequently, states did not have superintendent evaluation policies that contain any utility indicators at all. However, the second most frequent state utility standard score was six. This means that most states either scored very high or very low on the utility standard.

Table 3.7 presents the frequency of rubric scores for each indicator of the utility standard.

Table 3.7. Statewide Frequency of Rubric Scores by Indicator for the Utility Standard

Indicator	1	0.5	0
Data Collection Procedures: Evaluation Goals & Purposes			
Indicator A: Does the state identify a goal or purpose for superintendent evaluation?	14	3	17
Data Collection Procedures: Selected Performance Criteria & Measures			
Indicator B: Does the state mandate particular superintendent evaluation criteria or components?	18	5	11
Indicator C: Do the mandated criteria or components directly name any existing professional educational standards or reflect at least 75% of any existing professional educational standards even if such standards are not directly named?	10	1	23
Indicator D: Does the state identify evaluation components that specifically reference the goals or purpose for superintendent evaluation?	6	6	22
Indicator E: Does the state mandate inclusion of student progress measures in the superintendent evaluation?	10	8	16
Methods for Using Results			
Indicator F: Does the state mandate or permit superintendent contractual provisions based upon evaluation results?	8	2	24
Indicator G: Does the state mandate or permit evaluation results to be used for development of a professional growth plan (or similar document) or other human resource decisions?	9	11	14

Note: Thirty-four state scores are reflected; seventeen states did not have a policy and were not scored.

Four indicators or sets of indicators are worth noting in the utility standard:

1. **Evaluation Goals and Purposes** (*Indicator A*): Half of the states, seventeen of the thirty-four states with policies, identified goals and purposes for the superintendent evaluation. The vast majority of those states identified performance evaluation, professional development/growth, and setting expectations as the goals of superintendent evaluation. Notably, eight states identified either school improvement or accountability as one of the goals and purposes of the superintendent evaluation process. Though evaluations can be a positive means of improving board and superintendent relations/communications, only three states specifically listed board and superintendent relations/communication as a goal or purpose of superintendent evaluation. Quite interestingly, one state, North Carolina, identified integration with educational leader licensure and preparation as a goal or purpose for superintendent evaluation.

2. **Performance Criteria and Measures** (*Indicators B and E*): Twenty-three states identified either mandatory criteria (eighteen states) or permissive criteria (five states) for superintendent evaluations. It is clear that states were frequently including student progress measures within the identified criteria. Eighteen of the twenty-three states that identified performance criteria, included student progress measures as mandated criteria (ten states) or permissive criteria (eight states). These findings represented a substantial increase from DiPaola and Stronge's (2001b) research investigating the inclusion of student progress measures in superintendent evaluation policy. At that time, only three of fifty states included student progress measures in superintendent evaluation policy.

3. **Inclusion of Professional Standards as Criteria** (*Indicator C*): Only eleven of the twenty-three states either explicitly referenced professional standards or referenced standards that were substantially aligned with professional standards. In the eleven states where professional standards were referenced, states typically identified the standards as the state adopted standards for educational or school/district leaders with reference to or alignment with a set of professional standards. Professional standards referenced included AASA standards, NSBA standards, Professional Standards for Educational Leaders (PSEL), and Midcontinent Research for Education and Learning (McREL) standards. Though no clear majority could be discerned for the use of a particular professional standard, there was a slight majority toward the PSEL standards.

4. **Using Evaluation Results** (*Indicators F and G*): State superintendent evaluation policy indicated that some states linked superintendent evaluations to contractual decisions, but these states did not represent a majority. States more frequently linked superintendent evaluation results to professional development/growth decisions. In fact, in comparison, twice as

many states, twenty states, used evaluations for professional development/ growth decisions as compared to only ten states that used evaluations for contractual decisions.

A summary of each state's score on the utility standard by criteria, category, and indicator is contained in Appendix M.

Feasibility Standard. Overall, states exhibited mixed results for depth of policy on the feasibility standard, but with more depth than other standards. With only two indicators, the maximum total feasibility score for each state was only two. Approximately 79 percent (twenty-seven of thirty-four) of states with policies satisfied at least one indicator, but only five states satisfied both indicators.

There was a clear explanation for these results. A majority of the states with policies dictated the frequency of the superintendent evaluation (*Indicator A*), whereas only Delaware, Massachusetts, Michigan, New York, and Washington maintained a superintendent process data tracking system (*Indicator B*).

Table 3.8 presents the frequency of rubric scores for each indicator of the feasibility standard.

Table 3.8. Statewide Frequency of Rubric Scores by Indicator for the Feasibility Standard

Indicator	1	0.5	0
Data Collection Procedures: Frequency of Evaluation			
Indicator A: Does the state dictate frequency of superintendent evaluation?	25	2	7
Data Collection Procedures: Reporting			
Indicator B: Does the state maintain a superintendent process data tracking system? (i.e., Does the state require districts to report superintendent evaluation results to the state?)	5	0	29

Note: Thirty-four state scores are reflected; seventeen states did not have a policy and were not scored.

Though the feasibility standard only contained two indicators, both are worth discussion as they represent different ends of the scoring spectrum:

1. **Frequency of Evaluation** (*Indicator A*): States dictated that superintendent evaluation be conducted with some level of minimum frequency. Twenty-seven of the thirty-four states with policies had a provision that identified the timeframe and frequency of superintendent evaluation (*Indicator A*). All but two of those twenty-seven states mandated the frequency

rather than suggesting a particular frequency. Though the majority required an annual evaluation, a limited few provided for evaluations twice per year, like North Dakota, or provided for alternate frequencies for new or probationary superintendents.

2. **Superintendent Policy Data Tracking** (*Indicator B*): Overwhelmingly absent from state-level superintendent evaluation policy were state-level oversight mechanisms for tracking the superintendent evaluation process and reporting results. Only five of the thirty-four states with policies required any type of data tracking or reporting to the state. Recall in the propriety standard indicators, there was an indicator to determine a state's oversight of the superintendent evaluation process to ensure it was implemented with fidelity (propriety standard *Indicator C*), where only ten states had such oversight provisions. Here, even fewer reinforced that oversight with a data tracking process.

A summary of each state's score on the feasibility standard by criteria, category, and indicator is contained in Appendix M.

Accuracy Standard. Overall, states exhibited the least depth of policy on the accuracy standard, a standard with the greatest number of indicators and, therefore, the highest potential score. With ten indicators, the maximum total accuracy score for each state was ten. Yet despite this potential score, approximately 80 percent of states (twenty-seven of thirty-four states) with superintendent evaluation policies scored three or less on the accuracy standard.

Table 3.9 presents the frequency of rubric scores for each indicator of the accuracy standard.

Five indicators or sets of indicators are worth noting in the accuracy standard:

1. **Recognition of District-Specific Demographics** (*Indicators I and J*): Perhaps the largest contributor to the overall low accuracy standard scores was the absence of indicators in the category of system structure: recognition of district-specific demographics. Only one state, Missouri, had provisions that recognized differences in the type of district (rural, urban, suburban) and only two states, Massachusetts and North Carolina, had provisions that recognized differences in district demographics. North Carolina identified the demographic as limiting the superintendent evaluation policy components to superintendents serving in low-performing schools. Massachusetts recognized the resulting impact that demographics would have on the job duties of the superintendent.

2. **Evaluator Identification** (*Indicator D*): Every state that had a superintendent evaluation policy identified the evaluators for the superintendent

Table 3.9. Statewide Frequency of Rubric Scores by Indicator for the Accuracy Standard

Indicator	1	0.5	0
Data Collection Procedures: Data Integrity			
Indicator A: Does the state mandate that multiple sources of data must be used in the superintendent process?	8	6	20
Indicator B: Does the state assign different weights to different sources of superintendent evaluation data?	0	0	34
Indicator C: Does the state mandate a particular form for the superintendent evaluation?	3	13	18
Indicator D: Does the state identify evaluators for the superintendent evaluation?	34	0	0
Indicator E: Does the state mandate that multiple evaluator sources be used in the superintendent process?	9	6	19
Methods for Summarizing Results & System Evaluation			
Indicator F: Does the state mandate a process to assess the state-level superintendent evaluation system's effectiveness?	8	1	25
Indicator G: Did the state pilot the superintendent evaluation system model process or form?	2	1	31
Indicator H: Does the state identify outcomes to determine overall effectiveness of state-level superintendent evaluation system?	1	1	32
System Structure: Recognition of District-Specific Demographics			
Indicator I: Does the state differentiate between type of district (e.g., rural, urban, suburban) in the superintendent evaluation process?	0	1	33
Indicator J: Does the state differentiate between any district demographics in the superintendent evaluation process?	1	1	32

Note: Thirty-four state scores are reflected; seventeen states did not have a policy and were not scored.

evaluation. In fact, *Indicator D* was the only indicator, in any standard, that was met by every single state with a superintendent evaluation policy.

3. **Weighted Evaluation Criteria** (*Indicator B*): Not a single state assigned different weights to different evaluation criteria.

4. **Evaluation Form and Sources** (*Indicators C, A, and E*): While just short of a majority, fourteen states had provisions for multiple sources of data and fifteen states had provisions for multiple evaluation sources, and sixteen provided for either a mandated or permitted evaluation form in their superintendent evaluation policies. In this category, there was significant overlap among states. When states included these data integrity measures, they typically included all three of the measures. Specifically, eleven states included all three of these data integrity measures in their superintendent evaluation policies. These states included Delaware, Hawaii, Iowa, Massachusetts, Michigan, Mississippi, Missouri, New Jersey, North Carolina, Ohio, and Virginia.

5. **Evaluation System Effectiveness, Testing, and Outcomes** (*Indicators F, G, and H*): States varied in the inclusion of the indicators for the category of methods for summarizing results and system evaluation. Nine states identified a process to assess the state-level superintendent evaluation system's effectiveness. Despite this willingness of some states to assess the evaluation system process, very few states included provisions that would take steps to implement that assessment. Only three states piloted the superintendent evaluation system, and only two states identified outcomes to determine the superintendent evaluation system's effectiveness.

A summary of each state's score on the accuracy standard by criteria, category, and indicator is contained in Appendix M.

WHAT DOES THE CURRENT STATUS OF SUPERINTENDENT EVALUATION POLICY AT THE STATE LEVEL MEAN FOR PRACTICE?

It is a first step to understand the current status of superintendent evaluation policy at the state level. The next step is to determine the meaning and implications for superintendent evaluations in today's world.

States Are Ceding Superintendent Evaluation to Local Control

Despite the critical role of the superintendent to ensure successful district outcomes, a third of the states did not provide school districts with a superintendent evaluation policy, and eight states that did have policies still score three or less on the rubric. The practical effect is that these states are surrendering almost complete control to the local school district.

Leaving important superintendent performance evaluation processes to local control has significant implications. When boards of education and superintendents are left entirely to navigate this critical process on their own, there is potential for "political game playing" (Hoyle and Skrla, 1999, p. 405), potential for the deterioration of the board of education and superintendent relationship and the resulting breakdown of school district leadership, and potential for high superintendent turnover (Alsbury, 2008; Grady and Bryant, 1989).

The implications need not be as intentionally negative as "political game playing." Boards of education may want to implement a fair and effective superintendent evaluation process, but they simply do not know how. There is no requirement that board members have an educational background or knowledge of employee performance evaluations to serve on the board. They are representatives of the community, the public. Board members may want and need the direction that an informed, coherent state-level superintendent evaluation policy with sufficient depth can provide.

Certainly, the lack of state-level superintendent evaluation policy does not suggest that superintendents are not being evaluated in these states. States may have a practice of providing guidance to boards of education and superintendents, even if not in the form of statutory or regulatory policy. However, without a state-level superintendent policy, there is no guarantee that superintendents in these states are being evaluated at all. If they are being evaluated, there is no guarantee that superintendents in these states are consistently being evaluated fairly, equitably, and accurately, in a manner that produces useful results.

Superintendent Evaluation Policy May Fall Victim to the Principal Evaluation Policy Lag

Given that there is only a presumption that states are updating superintendent evaluation policies in the wake of the federal accountability and reform movement and given that there is the potential that states are just updating policies in accordance with a policy revision cycle, there continues to be a real concern that superintendent evaluation policy is not being given the attention it deserves. There is real potential, without more action in the way of superintendent evaluation policy development, that superintendent evaluation policy will potentially experience the ten-year lag faced by principal evaluation policy, if not an even longer lag.

One of the signals that principal evaluation policy was receiving meaningful attention and development that recognized and facilitated the principal's role in the accountability and reform movement was state legislative action to emphasize principal evaluation in conjunction with and in alignment with principal preparation and licensure (Jacques, Clifford, and Hornung, 2012). These research findings indicate such a signal is not yet present for superintendent evaluation policy.

The utility standard, *Indicator A*, where states identified the goals and purposes of superintendent evaluation policy, would be such a signal. Yet only North Carolina identified integration of evaluation, licensure, and preparation as one of the goals of the superintendent evaluation policy. Moreover, none of the current legislative efforts across states speak to the integration of district-level evaluation, licensure, and preparation (Scott, 2017).

States Have Not Placed Emphasis on Ensuring Evaluations Are Fair and Accurate

States scored low on the propriety standard. In practical terms, states have not placed much emphasis on ensuring that superintendent evaluations are fair and consider the welfare of the superintendent. Unfortunately, these findings implicate a pattern in that they are consistent with superintendent perceptions and prior research and serve as evidence that states are not doing enough to ensure that the unique intricacies of the superintendent evaluation process are adequately recognized and addressed in the superintendent evaluation process.

Superintendents reported that their evaluations do not recognize the full complexity of their role, perceived that they are not being evaluated accurately based on identified criteria (Kowalski et al., 2011; Mayo and McCartney, 2004), and were instead being evaluated by board member individual and subjective narratives (Costa, 2004; DiPaola, 2007). These findings are also consistent with DiPaola and Stronge's (2001b) research as to the accuracy standard. Almost twenty years ago, DiPaola and Stronge found that the criteria most absent from superintendent evaluation policies were the accuracy standard, and the findings of this study show that the accuracy standard continues to be neglected.

Study results further confirm that states are not taking adequate steps to ensure the propriety standard is met through exclusion of evaluators with conflicts of interest and who are untrained. Not a single state mandated the exclusion of evaluators with conflicts of interest, and only ten states required training for board member evaluators. In a performance evaluation process where the evaluators are a group of public representatives with no required education background or required background in employee performance evaluation, board members typically will not know to exclude themselves if they have a conflict of interest and will not know how to implement a fair, accurate evaluation process.

In fact, some board members will run for office on platforms that specifically seek to remove the superintendent. When elected, those same board members seek to evaluate the superintendent without considering the lack of impartiality and the resulting conflict of interest. It is within this aspect of the propriety standard where there is most significant potential for political influence and the breakdown of the board member and superintendent relationship.

Certainly, not all board members act with ill intention. With high board member turnover and state law that limit board member terms of office, many board members are simply too new and untrained to recognize the right path and process for superintendent evaluation. States would benefit from incorporating provisions similar to West Virginia's policy that provides for a balanced, jointly developed training by the state affiliates of both professional administrator and board member associations.

States also scored low on the accuracy standards. In practical terms, states have not placed much emphasis on ensuring that superintendent evaluations are justified, well documented, and logically linked to data sources. States are not taking adequate steps to ensure superintendent evaluation processes recognize role differences related to district-specific demographics.

Only one state, Missouri, differentiated the superintendent evaluation process by type of district (e.g., rural, urban, suburban), and did so permissibly. Likewise, only two states, Massachusetts and North Carolina, differentiated by the district demographic of student enrollment, North Carolina mandatorily and Massachusetts permissibly. Research conducted by DiPaola (2010), DiPaola and Stronge (2001b), and Jones and Howley (2009) link differences in district type, student enrollment, and district socioeconomic status to differences in the superintendent's role, responsibilities, and performance expectations.

The impact of a state's failure to differentiate by district-specific demographics cannot be understated. Not only is the accountability and reform movement changing the role and performance expectations for superintendents, such changes are not felt in the same way by every superintendent in every district. The context of a superintendent's role is relevant to performance expectations, the resulting impact of accountability and reform expectations, and even position longevity (The Broad Center, 2018).

Examples can be found in any state, but take Pennsylvania to illustrate. A superintendent in Philadelphia, Pennsylvania, an urban school district educating almost 135,000 students with low socioeconomic status, will have drastically different job duties and performance expectations than a superintendent in Thornburg, Pennsylvania, a suburban/rural school district educating less than one hundred students with high socioeconomic status.

The Philadelphia superintendent may focus more on managerial tasks and external relationships to secure funding, whereas the Thornburg superintendent may focus more on developing a culture of professional learning and instructional leadership. It is equally possible that expectations of the accountability and reform movement may force the Philadelphia superintendent to take a more active role in developing a culture of professional learning and instructional leadership.

State-level superintendent evaluation policy, to be effective, must recognize district demographic differences and the resulting superintendent role and provide a mechanism to shift with external demands. It is not evident that the states are making such policy distinctions.

Several findings have particularly noteworthy implications related to the use of particular performance criteria and related to superintendent evaluation implementation at the local level. Such implications are particularly relevant, so much that we felt it appropriate to dedicate entire chapters toward these topics. We will discuss performance criteria in chapter 4 and implementation in chapter 6.

States Must Focus Continued Emphasis on Formative and Summative Evaluation Components

Frequency of evaluation points to the importance placed on superintendent evaluation process and serves as evidence of whether boards of education are ensuring evaluations are using both midyear formative in addition to summative components (Kowalski et al., 2011). Twenty-five of the thirty-four states with policies mandated the frequency of superintendent evaluations with another two states permissively identifying the frequency of evaluation. However, twenty-four of those twenty-five states mandated that frequency as occurring annually. Only one state mandated evaluations twice per year. This suggests that superintendent evaluations, despite any stated purposes, are designed with a summative purpose rather than including a formative purpose.

Efforts should be made to increase the frequency of superintendent evaluation to provide for the beneficial outcomes using both formative and summative components. As the findings suggest, twenty states indicate that superintendent evaluation results are used for professional growth. If that is truly the case, states should consider adopting a requirement for more frequent, formative evaluation processes.

Summary

Even in the wake of the federal accountability and reform movement, the federal government has not acted to govern superintendent evaluation. Given the absence of federal regulation over superintendent evaluation, conceptual soundness of the evaluation is left to state control. That responsibility is passed along to local control when states choose not to act. A review of state-level superintendent evaluation policy across the fifty states and Washington, DC, found that seventeen states do not have a superintendent evaluation policy. Thus, these states continue to pass along responsibility to local control. The remaining states displayed a loose pattern of policy development aligned with the federal accountability movement. The remaining states also displayed mixed coherence with the JCSEE standards, with less depth on propriety and accuracy standards.

REFERENCES

Alsbury, T. L. (2008). School board member and superintendent turnover and the influence on student achievement: An application of dissatisfaction theory. *Leadership and Policy in Schools*, 7, 202–29. doi:10.1080/15700760701748428.

American Institutes for Research. (2018). Databases on state teacher and principal evaluation policies [webpage]. Retrieved from http://resource.tqsource.org/stateevaldb/.

Björk, L. G., Browne-Ferrigno, T., and Kowalski, T. J. (2014). The superintendent and educational reform in the United States of America. *Leadership and Policy in Schools*, 13, 444–65. doi:10.1080/15700763.2014.945656.

Boyd, W. L. (1976). The public, the professionals, and educational policy making: Who governs? *Teachers College Record*, 77, 539–77.

Cohen, D. K., Spillane, J. P., and Peurach, D. J. (2018). The dilemmas of educational reform. *Educational Researcher*, 47, 204–12. doi:10.3102/0013189X17743488.

Costa, E. W., II. (2004). Performance-based evaluations for superintendents: Combining formative and summative approaches to address procedures, policies, and products. *School Administrator*, 61(9). Retrieved from http://www.aasa.org/SchoolAdministratorArticle.aspx?id=10250.

DiPaola, M. F. (2007). Revisiting superintendent evaluation. *School Administrator*, 64(6).

DiPaola, M. F. (2010). Evaluating the superintendent [White paper]. Retrieved from American Association of School Administrators website: http://www.aasa.org/uploadedFiles/Resources/AASA_White_Paper_on_Superintendent_Evaluation.pdf.

DiPaola, M. F., and Stronge, J. H. (2001a). Credible evaluation: Not yet state-of-the-art. *School Administrator*, 58(2), 18–21.

DiPaola, M. F., and Stronge, J. H. (2001b). Superintendent evaluation in a standards-based environment: A status report from the states. *Journal of Personnel Evaluation in Education*, 15, 97–110.

DiPaola, M. F., and Stronge, J. H. (2003). *Superintendent evaluation handbook*. Lanham, MD: Scarecrow Press.

Elementary and Secondary Education Act as amended by the Every Student Succeeds Act, 20 U.S.C. §6301 et seq. (2015).

Finnan, L. A., McCord, R. S., Stream, C. C., Mattocks, T. C., Peterson, G. J., and Ellerson, N. M. (2015). *Study of the American superintendent: 2015 mid-decade update*. Alexandria, VA: American Association of School Administrators.

Fowler, F. C. (2013). *Policy studies for educational leaders: An introduction*. Upper Saddle River, NJ: Pearson Education.

Grady, M. L., and Bryant, M. T. (1989). Critical incidents between superintendents and school boards: Implications for practice. *Planning and Changing*, 20, 206–14.

Henrikson, R. (2018). Superintendent evaluation frameworks for continuous school improvement: Using evidence-based practices to promote the stance of improvement. *AASA Journal of Scholarship and Practice*, 15(1), 22–29.

Hoyle, J., and Skrla, L. (1999). The politics of superintendent evaluation. *Journal of Personnel Evaluation in Education*, 13(4), 405–19.

Jacques, C., Clifford, M., and Hornung, K. (2012). *Principal evaluation policy landscape: A survey of state policies*. Washington, DC: Center on Great Teachers and Leaders.

Joint Committee on Standards for Educational Evaluation. (1988). *The personnel evaluation standards*. Newbury Park, CA: Sage.

Joint Committee on Standards for Educational Evaluation. (2009). *The personnel evaluation standards* (second ed.). Newbury Park, CA: Sage.

Jones, K., and Howley, A. (2009). Contextual influences on superintendents' time usage. *Education Policy Analysis Archives*, 17(23), 1–24.

Keedy, J. L., and Björk, L. G. (2002). Superintendents and local boards and the potential for community polarization: The call for use of political strategist skills. In B. S. Cooper and L. D. Fusarelli (Eds.), *The promises and perils facing today's school superintendent* (pp. 103–27). Lanham, MD: Scarecrow Press.

Kowalski, T. J., McCord, R. S., Peterson, G. J., Young, I. P., and Ellerson, N. M. (2011). *The American school superintendent 2010 decennial study*. Lanham, MD: Rowman & Littlefield Education.

Kraft, M. E., and Furlong, S. R. (2018). *Public policy: Politics, analysis, and alternatives*. Thousand Oaks, CA: CQ Press.

Learning Forward. (2017). A new vision for professional learning: A toolkit to help states advance learning and improvement systems. Retrieved from https://learningforward.org/docs/default-source/getinvolved/essa/essanewvisiontoolkit.

Marzano, R. J., and Waters, T. (2009). *District leadership that works: Striking the right balance*. Bloomington, IN: Solution Tree Press.

Mayo, C. R., and McCartney, G. P. (2004). School superintendents' evaluations: Effective and results-based? *ERS Spectrum*, 22(1), 19–33.

Parker, J. (1995, August–September). *Politics, culture, and education Goals 2000: The politics of systemic education reform in the American states*. Paper presented at the Annual Meeting of the American Political Science Association, Chicago, IL. Retrieved from ERIC database (ED392688).

Reeves, D. B. (2008). *Assessing educational leaders: Evaluating performance for improved individual and organizational results*. Thousand Oaks, CA: Corwin Press.

Schneider, T. L. (2019). A state-level superintendent evaluation policy analysis (Doctoral dissertation). Retrieved from ProQuest Dissertations and Theses (10977630).

Scott, D. (2017). 2017 state policy review: School and district leadership. Denver, CO: Education Commission of the States. Retrieved from https://www.ecs.org/wp-content/uploads/2017-State-Policy-Review-School-and-district-leadership.pdf.

The Broad Center. (2018). Hire expectations: Big-district superintendents stay in their jobs longer than we think. Retrieved from https://www.broadcenter.org/wp-content/uploads/2018/05/TheBroadCenter_HireExpectations_May2018.pdf.

Chapter Four

Performance Standards

The Foundation for Superintendent Evaluation

The foundation of an effective performance evaluation system in education, including for superintendents, is the use of clearly described and well-documented performance standards. In order for an evaluation to be fair and comprehensive, it is necessary to describe the standards for superintendents with sufficient detail and accuracy so that both the superintendent and those evaluating her or him can reasonably understand the expectations of the job.

In essence, what performance standards do is guarantee that the superintendent is evaluated based on what she or he was hired to do! And, in so doing, the job standards serve as the cornerstone of the performance evaluation system.

In this chapter, the processes and products related to the design of the superintendent's performance standards are explored. The model presented is fashioned from Stronge's (2012) work done for the Commonwealth of Virginia.

In particular, the following questions are addressed:

1. What are performance standards?
2. How can superintendent performance standards be used in building an evaluation system in a specific school district setting?
3. What is the relationship between the superintendent performance standards and other standards?
4. What is the relationship between the superintendent performance standards and the superintendent's job description?

WHAT ARE PERFORMANCE STANDARDS?

While various approaches could be employed to describe the job of the superintendent, this evaluation system is based on a three-tiered description of performance:

DOMAINS
Performance Standards
Performance Indicators

Textbox 4.1.   *Source:* DiPaola and Stronge, 2003

Domains

Domains reflect the framework for describing major aspects of the work of educators. Basically, domains are categories of job expectations and serve as logical clusters for those job expectations. In other words, domains are categories or placeholders for the superintendent's specific performance standards. The domains provide the framework for describing the major aspects of the job.

We have included a model for consideration of seven domains for superintendents. As presented in figure 4.1, this role description is based on a combination of a sociopolitical and a functional perspective of the superintendent's role.

Performance Standards

Performance standards are the job responsibilities or duties performed by an educator. They provide greater specification of role expectations but are still broader in nature than discrete, observable behaviors. Performance standards are the duties performed by a superintendent. They are organized within the seven general domains.

Performance indicators also are intended to provide greater clarity on the precise nature of the domain but do not provide a specific behavior or set of behaviors that would be directly amenable to assessment. They clarify specific portions of the domain but are not specific, observable behaviors or actions. An example of a superintendent performance standard within the domain of Instructional Leadership is listed below (textbox 4.2).

Recommended Superintendent Evaluation Domains	AASA Professional Standards							
	Communications and Community Relations	Human Resources Management	Leadership and District Culture	Curriculum Planning and Development	Instructional Management	Policy and Governance	Organizational Management	Values and Ethics of Leadership
Policy and Governance	✓					✓		
Planning and Assessment	✓	✓	✓	✓	✓	✓	✓	
Instructional Leadership	✓		✓	✓	✓	✓		✓
Organizational Management	✓	✓	✓		✓	✓	✓	
Communications and Community Relations	✓		✓	✓		✓	✓	✓
Professionalism	✓		✓			✓		✓

Figure 4.1. **Superintendency Matrix Comparing the Recommended Domains and AASA Professional Standards**

A complete set of superintendent performance standards, organized by the seven previously identified domains, is provided in Appendix A.

Performance Indicators

Performance indicators are used in the superintendent's evaluation system to do just what the term *implies—indicate* in observable behaviors the types and quality of performance associated with the major job responsibilities (performance standards). Performance indicators constitute the most specific description of performance standards in the three-tiered hierarchy and lend themselves nicely to documentation and direct assessment.

Typically, there will be two to six performance indicators used to define each performance standard. However, it is important to note that performance indicators are typically *not* used as the unit of evaluation; rather, they are provided to highlight what a superintendent would do if she or he were properly fulfilling the job requirement.

Examples of performance indicators for the superintendent Instructional Leadership standard L-1 (textbox 4.2) are listed in textbox 4.3.

Textbox 4.2. Superintendent Performance Standard L-1

The superintendent communicates a clear vision of excellence and continuous improvement consistent with the goals of the school district. (Sample performance standard L-1)

Textbox 4.3. Sample Performance Indicators for Standard L-1

The superintendent . . .

- Communicates a clear vision of excellence and continuous improvement consistent with the goals of the school system.
- Directs staff to set specific and challenging, but attainable, goals for higher performance that result in improved student learning.
- Oversees the alignment, coordination, and delivery of assigned programs and curricular areas so that the school district and all schools in it meet all required federal, state, and local standards.
- Assesses factors affecting student achievement and directs change for needed improvements.
- Ensures that curricular design, instructional strategies, and learning environments integrate appropriate technologies to maximize student learning.
- Explores, disseminates, and applies knowledge and information about new or improved instructional strategies or related issues.

Performance indicators such as these have been developed for each performance standard. The sample performance indicators are not intended to be all, inclusive lists but rather examples of typical behaviors that indicate satisfactory performance of the applicable standard by a superintendent.

In summary, performance indicators:

- Are the observable activities that relate to the performance of the job responsibilities
- Are representative of a particular job responsibility
- Can be objectively documented and measured
- Are intended merely as samples and not as a full set of behaviors for any job

A set of suggested superintendent performance indicators, along with domains and performance standards, is located in Appendix A.

HOW CAN SUPERINTENDENT PERFORMANCE STANDARDS BE USED IN BUILDING AN EVALUATION IN A SPECIFIC SCHOOL DISTRICT SETTING?

Domains, the first tier used in defining the job of superintendents, identify major categories of work, and *performance indicators*, the third tier, serve as examples of behaviors that will be observed or documented. However, it is the *performance standards* that are the basic building blocks of the evaluation system.

In most performance evaluation systems, the performance standards are viewed as the explicit job requirements for the superintendent, and all applicable standards must be fulfilled in order to meet job expectations. Remember, for summative evaluation ratings, superintendents typically are evaluated on each standard. In some instances, school boards prefer to give an aggregate or overall rating for the major domains. However, the performance indicators definitely should not be used for summative ratings as they are intended merely to serve as suggested activities and behaviors that shed light on the performance standards.

The list of superintendent performance standards included in this book are intended to be as comprehensive as possible. However, we do *not* intend that an entire list be implemented verbatim because—

- In order for one person to implement all of the duties identified for a position in any meaningful fashion, it would require the proverbial 110 percent effort. In most cases it just isn't practical nor is it productive to attempt to do everything.
- Even if it *is* feasible to implement all of the identified performance standards, it probably isn't desirable. Expectations and needs vary from one organization to another, and even within the same school district there frequently is the need to refocus or redefine the job from time to time. This factor needs to be considered in designing the superintendent's job and selecting the specific performance standards to be emphasized.
- The context of the job needs to be considered when defining it. For example, some of the performance standards listed for the superintendent may be more appropriate in some school districts than in others. The performance standards included in the performance evaluation should reflect these differences in assignment from school district to school district.

WHAT IS THE RELATIONSHIP BETWEEN THE
SUPERINTENDENT PERFORMANCE EVALUATION
STANDARDS AND OTHER GUIDELINES?

When the seven domains were created, careful consideration was given to how well they fit with existing professional guidelines and standards related to superintendent work. In particular to:

- The AASA's professional standards for the superintendency (1993)
- The roles of the superintendent as identified by the NSBA (Gemberling, Smith, and Villani, 2000)
- The Professional Standards for Educational Leaders (National Policy Board for Educational Administration, 2015)
- Technology Standards for School Administrators (TSSA Collaborative, 2001)

American Association of School Administrators
Recommended Standards

In an effort to define the profession of the superintendency, AASA established a commission that developed a set of eight professional standards and a corresponding set of competencies (AASA, 1993). The commission stated that "all superintendents should be held accountable for the eight professional standards" (Carter and Cunningham, 1997, p. 17).

Further, in 1998, AASA published skills/standards for successful twenty-first-century school leaders (Hoyle, English, and Steffy, 1998). The AASA standards consist of the eight interrelated standards as depicted in textbox 4.4.

National School Boards Association Recommended Standards

In 2000, the NSBA published a guide to assist local school boards in focusing efforts on their key work—increasing student progress (Gemberling et al., 2000). The authors of the NSBA book argue that this systemic approach results in high-quality schools with student progress as their primary focus. The guide defines the roles of both the board and superintendent in each of eight "key action areas" that include:

- Vision
- Standards
- Assessment
- Accountability

Textbox 4.4. Descriptions of Superintendent Performance Domains

1. Mission, Vision, and Goals
The superintendent works with the local school board to formulate and implement the school division's mission, vision, and goals to promote student progress.
2. Planning and Assessment
The superintendent strategically gathers, analyzes, and uses a variety of data to guide planning and decision making consistent with established guidelines, policies, and procedures that result in student progress.
3. Instructional Leadership
The superintendent fosters the success of all teachers, staff, and students by ensuring the development, communication, implementation, and evaluation of effective teaching and learning that leads to student progress and school improvement.
4. Organizational Leadership and Safety
The superintendent fosters the safety and success of all teachers, staff, and students by supporting, managing, and evaluating the division's organization, operation, and use of resources.
5. Communication and Community Relations
The superintendent fosters the success of all students through effective engagement of and communication with stakeholders.
6. Professionalism
The superintendent fosters the success of teachers, staff, and students by demonstrating professional standards and ethics, engaging in continuous professional development, and contributing to the profession.
7. District Student Progress
The superintendent's leadership results in acceptable, measurable division wide student progress based on established standards.

- Alignment
- Climate
- Collaboration
- Continuous improvement (Gemberling et al., 2000)

Interstate School Leaders Licensure Consortium Recommended Standards

The Professional Standards for Educational Leaders (PSEL) developed by The National Policy Board for Educational Administration (NPBEA, 2015) are grounded in current research and the real-life experiences of educational leaders. The PSELs are foundational to all levels of educational leadership.

The PSEL are "model" professional standards that communicate expectations to practitioners, supporting institutions, professional associations, policy makers, and the public about the work, qualities, and values of effective educational leaders. The standards reflect interdependent domains, qualities, and values of leadership work that research and practice suggest are integral to student progress and success:

1. Mission, Vision, and Core Values
2. Ethics and Professional Norms
3. Equity and Cultural Responsiveness
4. Curriculum, Instruction, and Assessment
5. Community of Care and Support for Students
6. Professional Capacity of School Personnel
7. Professional Community for Teachers and Staff
8. Meaningful Engagement of Families and Community
9. Operations and Management
10. School Improvement (NPBEA, 2015)

International Society for Technology Education Recommended Standards

Recognizing the need for technology standards for school administrators, the AASA, NSBA, other national school administrator organizations, and the International Society for Technology Education formed a collaborative to develop standards. The standards define the specifics of what superintendents and other school administrators "need to know and be able to do in order to discharge their responsibility as leaders in the effective use of technology in our schools" (TSSA Collaborative, 2001, p. 1).

Standards and performance indicators are contained in a framework of six major areas, including:

- Leadership and vision
- Learning and teaching
- Productivity and professional practice
- Support, management, and operations
- Assessment and evaluation
- Social, legal, and ethical issues

Comparing the Recommended Standards

Using a framework of administrator skills (Katz, 1955), we compared the four sets of national standards by categorizing the individual standards within each set according to the category of leadership skills required to meet each standard (table 4.1). When preparation programs for superintendents are aligned with these four sets of standards, the development of technical skills and acquiring specialized knowledge are emphasized, as well as the conceptual and human skills that dominate the leadership literature.

Table 4.1. American Association of School Administrators Superintendent Standards

MSA Standard	Key Descriptors
Standard 1: Leadership and District Culture	Vision, academic rigor, excellence, empowerment, problem solving
Standard 2: Policy and Governance	Policy formulation, democratic processes, regulations
Standard 3: Communications and Community Relations	Internal and external communications, community support, consensus building
Standard 4: Organizational Management	Data-driven decision making, problem solving, operations management, and reporting
Standard 5: Curriculum Planning and Development	Curriculum planning, instructional design, human growth, and development
Standard 6: Instructional Management	Student progress, classroom management, instructional technology
Standard 7: Human Resources Management	Personnel induction, development, evaluation, compensation, organizational health
Standard 8: Values and Ethics of Leadership	Multicultural and ethnic understanding, personal integrity, and ethics

The Match between the Superintendent Evaluation Domains and AASA Standards

While the national standards provide a framework for defining the role of the superintendent, it should be noted that the standards tend to reflect generic superintendent duties and responsibilities (DiPaola and Stronge, 2001a). As Carter and Cunningham (1997) noted, the divergent interests and expectations that exist in each school district thwart attempts to standardize criteria for superintendent evaluation. While the standards may only be a general guide, they can be very useful in bringing the board and superintendent together to tailor evaluation criteria to fit the local district (Horler, 1996).

Checklists with details for all eight AASA standards and accompanying indicators are provided in Appendix A. The checklists can be used to assess how well a job description correlates with the AASA standards. Additionally, they can be helpful in aligning a superintendent's evaluation instrument with the standards.

Figure 4.1 depicts the relationship between the recommended superintendent evaluation domains that we identify in this book (Appendix B) and the AASA standards. You will note that we have condensed the AASA standards from eight to six domains for the purposes of designing a performance evaluation system.

WHAT IS THE RELATIONSHIP BETWEEN THE SUPERINTENDENT PERFORMANCE STANDARDS AND THE SUPERINTENDENT'S JOB DESCRIPTION?

Local school boards traditionally have defined the responsibilities of the superintendent in terms of a job description—a general description that frequently is related only loosely to actual job responsibilities. Additionally, the job description typically is even more loosely connected to the superintendent's evaluation (DiPaola and Stronge, 2001a, 2001b).

Most superintendents do have a job description, but in *The 2000 Study of the American Superintendency*, only 50.2 percent stated that they are evaluated according to the criteria in the job description (Glass, Bjork, and Brunner, 2000). In our discussion of the superintendent's performance evaluation, what is important is that the job description:

- Be an accurate general description of the superintendent's role
- Serve as a useful guide in advertising and selecting a superintendent
- Serve as a basis upon which the superintendent's evaluation can be built
- Be rationally connected to the specific duties and responsibilities contained within the superintendent's performance evaluation

Figure 4.1 demonstrates the use of language that typically is included in a superintendent job description. We recommend that the school board and superintendent thoughtfully consider the relationship between the job description and the evaluation when developing or revising them.

This process is especially important in negotiating a new contract. If the two documents have been properly aligned, it can smooth communications later and help both parties avoid potential misunderstandings.

SUPERINTENDENT PERFORMANCE CRITERIA
AND STUDENT ACHIEVEMENT

In chapter 2 we stated that in 2000, local boards and board members across the nation "heard" the public concern related to student progress, and the NSBA proclaimed that the "key work" of school boards was improving student progress (Gemberling, Smith, and Villani, 2000, p. 1). In chapter 3, we acknowledged that the words of this proclamation have been incorporated into a number of state-level superintendent evaluation policies (Schneider, 2019). Such words, however, have a much farther-reaching impact in practice and, in the context of evaluation, cannot be considered in a vacuum.

Given that the superintendent is ultimately responsible for all district outcomes, including student progress outcomes, it is not surprising that this performance measure is being incorporated into all educational leader evaluation systems. However, states must carefully select performance criteria in a process that involves superintendents, board members, and professional associations.

This is particularly true with student progress, as such measures of progress impact a superintendent's tenure as superintendent in a state (Plotts and Gutmore, 2014) and in a district (Simpson, 2013). The superintendent's role in ensuring improved student progress outcomes may be more accurately described as having an indirect effect on instruction via instructional resource management, instructional policy support, and the balancing of internal and external political influences on instruction (Browne-Ferrigno and Glass, 2005; Hoyle et al., 2005; Waters and Marzano, 2006).

Thus, some superintendents would argue against the inclusion of student progress measures or any evaluation measures over which the superintendent does not have direct control. Other superintendents would argue for inclusion of the proper progress measures that accurately reflect that for which the superintendent can be held responsible.

Careful selection of performance criteria requires development of a collaborative process that includes superintendents, boards of education, and professional associations. Such a collaborative process will ensure superintendent performance criteria fairly and accurately reflects the superintendent's role and performance expectations.

Properly defining and understanding the superintendent's role in student progress and instructional leadership has significant implications not only when used as an evaluation criterion but also it has significant implications for a state's use of multiple data sources and the frequency of evaluation. Any well-formed performance evaluation system will ensure the use of multiple data sources. However, this is, perhaps, even more critical when considering

Table 4.2. Comparing Leadership Standards

	Technical Skills (special knowledge, enterprise as a whole)	Conceptual Skills (ability to see the ethical dimensions)	Human Skills (working with people, tools, and techniques)
ISLLC Standards (Interstate School Leaders Licensure Consortium)	Organizational management	Ability to develop and sustain culture Ability to develop and implement vision Understand and respond within large context	Collaborations with families and community Integrity and ethical behavior
AASA Standards for the Superintendency (American Association of School Administrators)	Policy and governance Organizational management Curriculum planning Instructional management Human resources management	Leadership and district culture	Communications and community relations Values and ethics
National Technology Standards for School Administrators (TSSA Collaborative)	Curriculum and instruction integrate appropriate technologies Apply technologies to enhance practice and productivity Provide support for integration and infrastructure Plan and implement effective assessments	Create vision for comprehensive integration of technology	Decisions reflect social, legal, ethical, and technology issues
NSBA Key Work (National School Boards Association)	Planning Curriculum alignment, instruction, and assessment focused on standards Accountability	Establish and maintain a positive climate Focus on continuous improvement	Build collaborative relations

the superintendent's indirect influence on student progress and the changing nature of state definitions of student progress.

Using multiple measures will more accurately define the superintendent's connection to and responsibility for student progress. This will maximize the accuracy and utility of the evaluation results while minimizing the potential harm to superintendents by seeking to hold them accountable for that which they do not directly control. Further, these multiple data sources related to student progress will have the most impact when used in a formative evaluation process.

Currently, states are requiring only an annual summative evaluation. Typical student progress outcomes are measured annually. It is difficult, if not impossible, to hold superintendents accountable in an accurate and meaningful way for performance data that is only measured annually. Instead, multiple data sources should be reviewed at multiple points throughout the year in a formative way to underscore the fairness, accuracy, and utility of the superintendent evaluation process (Schneider, 2019).

When these three indicators (use of student progress measures as an evaluation criterion, use of multiple data sources, and frequency of evaluation) are taken together, states have an opportunity to reinforce their philosophy of instructional leadership and the accountability of educational leaders (Maranto, Trivitt, Nichols, and Watson, 2017) through superintendent evaluation policy (Schneider, 2019). If states do not consider these elements together and incorporate them into the superintendent evaluation policy process (Schneider, 2019), local boards of education can misunderstand, or worse, misuse, student progress measures to unfairly target superintendents or engage in "political game playing" (Hoyle and Skrla, 1999, p. 405).

SUMMARY

In summary, we contend that a comprehensive and productive superintendent evaluation system is founded squarely upon clearly stated and clearly communicated job responsibilities (see textbox 4.5). If the role of the superintendent can be adequately described in the form of performance standards (as presented in Appendix B), then all parties can:

- *Know* what are the key performance expectations
- *Assess* actual performance based on the standards
- Fairly *judge* success based on objective criteria
- *Make* informed *decisions* for improvement

Textbox 4.5. **Sample Superintendent Job Description**

TITLE: Superintendent of Schools

PRIMARY FUNCTIONS:
The superintendent of schools provides educational leadership and administers the school district, in compliance with all School Board policies, state codes, and mandates set forth by the State Board of Education through the State Department of Education. The superintendent serves as the chief administrative officer of the school district and is responsible for:
1. General school administration
2. Instructional programs and services
3. Personnel leadership and supervision
4. Business and fiscal operations
5. School facilities management
6. Pupil transportation
7. Record keeping and reporting
8. Community relations

QUALIFICATIONS:
Possesses certification and qualifications as set forth by the State Board of Education. Possesses professional qualifications and personal attributes as set forth by the School Board.

EVALUATION:
The superintendent shall be evaluated at least annually by the School Board.

AUTHORITY RELATIONSHIPS:
The superintendent of schools is a constitutional state office through which the State Board of Education and Superintendent of Public Instruction exercise their supervision and control of the school district. The superintendent serves as the chief executive officer of the School Board and is responsible for enforcing all board policies. All personnel employed by the School Board answer, through proper channels, to the superintendent of schools.

REFERENCES

American Association of School Administrators. (1993). *Professional standards for the superintendency.* Arlington, VA: Author.

Browne-Ferrigno, T., and Glass, T. E. (2005). Superintendent as organizational manager. In L. G. Björk and T. J. Kowalski (Eds.), *The contemporary superintendent: Preparation, practice, and development* (pp. 137–61). Thousand Oaks, CA: Corwin Press.

Carter, G. R., and Cunningham, W. G. (1997). *The American school superintendent: Leading in an age of pressure.* San Francisco, CA: Jossey-Bass.

DiPaola, M. F. (2007). Revisiting superintendent evaluation. *School Administrator*, 64(6).

DiPaola, M. F. (2010). Evaluating the superintendent. [White Paper]. Retrieved February 8, 2018, from American Association of School Administrators http://www.aasa.org/uploadedFiles/Resources/AASA_White_Paper_on_Superintendent_Evaluation.pdf.

DiPaola, M. F., and Stronge, J. H. (2001a). Credible evaluation: Not yet state-of-the-art. *The School Administrator*, 58(2), 18–21.

DiPaola, M. D., and Stronge, J. H. (2001b). Superintendent evaluation in a standards-based environment: A status report from the states. *Journal of Personnel Evaluation in Education*, 15(2), 97–110.

Gemberling, K. W., Smith, C. W., and Villani, J. S. (2000). *The keywork of school boards guidebook*. Alexandria, VA: National School Boards Association.

Glass, T. E., Bjork, L., and Brunner, C. C. (2000). *The 2000 study of the American school superintendency*. Arlington, VA: American Association of School Administrators.

Horler, B. (1996). *A comparison of criteria used in the evaluation of the superintendency in Illinois as perceived by school board presidents and public school superintendents*. Unpublished doctoral dissertation, Northern Illinois University, DeKalb.

Hoyle, J. R., Bjork, L. G., Collier, V., and Glass, T. (2005). *The superintendent as CEO: Standards-based performance*. Thousand Oaks, CA: Corwin Press.

Hoyle, J. R., English, F. W., and Steffy, B. E. (1998). *Skills for successful 21st century school leaders: Standards for peak performers*. Arlington, VA: American Association of School Administrators.

Hoyle, J., and Skrla, L. (1999). The politics of superintendent evaluation. *Journal of Personnel Evaluation in Education*, 13(4), 405–19.

Katz, R. L. (1955). Skills of an effective administrator. *Harvard Business Review*, 3.3(1), 33–42.

Maranto, R., Trivitt, J., Nichols, M., and Watson, A. (2017). No contractual obligation to improve education: School boards and their superintendents. *Politics and Policy*, 45, 1003–23.

National Policy Board for Educational Administration (2015). *Professional standards for educational leaders 2015*. Reston, VA: Author.

Plotts, T., and Gutmore, D. (2014). The superintendent's influence on student achievement. *AASA Journal of Scholarship and Practice*, 11(1), 26–34.

Schneider, T. L. (2019). A state-level superintendent evaluation policy analysis (Doctoral dissertation). Retrieved from ProQuest Dissertations and Theses. (10977630).

Simpson, J. (2013). Superintendent tenure and student achievement. *Journal of Scholarship and Practice*, 9(4), 10–23.

Stronge, J. H. (2012). *Guidelines for uniform performance standards and evaluation criteria for superintendents*. Richmond, VA: Virginia Department of Education.

Technology Standards for School Administrators Collaborative. (2001). *Technology standards for school administrators (TSSA)*. Naperville, IL: North Regional Technology in Education Consortium.

Waters, T., and Marzano, R. J. (2006). *School district leadership that works: The effect of superintendent leadership on student achievement.* Denver, CO: Mid-continent Research for Education and Learning Laboratory.

Chapter Five

Documenting the Superintendent's Performance

As discussed in chapter 4, the foundation of an effective superintendent performance evaluation system is a comprehensive set of performance standards. However, the set of performance standards alone isn't adequate to ensure a quality evaluation system.

While the performance standards describe *what* the superintendent is expected to do, evaluators also need to know *how* the superintendent fulfills her or his work as well as *how well* the work is done. In other words, a quality performance evaluation system will provide ways and means for documenting the superintendent's performance and then offer a rubric for fairly judging that performance.

In this chapter, both the *how* and the *how well* aspects needed for designing and implementing a superintendent performance evaluation system are explored. Specifically, the following questions are addressed:

1. What are appropriate information sources for documenting the superintendent's performance?
2. How can the various information sources be integrated?
3. How is a scoring rubric used?
4. How can a superintendent scoring rubric be helpful in judging the superintendent's effectiveness?

WHAT ARE APPROPRIATE INFORMATION SOURCES FOR DOCUMENTING THE SUPERINTENDENT'S PERFORMANCE?

The role of superintendent requires a performance evaluation system that acknowledges the complexities of the job. It isn't enough to rely on opinion based on limited informal observations, recent events, and anecdotal evidence. In fact, such an approach to evaluate the superintendent will almost always:

- Allow uneven influence by a few constituents
- Provide only limited evidence of achievement
- Be based more on speculation than actual performance data
- Be subjective and founded upon opinion
- Result in an evaluation that is counterproductive to growth and improvement

In order to develop a complete picture of a superintendent's contribution to the overall success of the school system, the board of education should use multiple broad-based sources of information. These data sources might include informal observations, client surveys, artifacts of performance or portfolios, professional goals, student progress, and other relevant sources of information.

Systematically documenting performance in a variety of settings using a variety of means enhances the breadth and depth of both the superintendent's and the board's understanding of performance strengths and weaknesses. However, for data sources to be acceptable, they must meet the tests of logic, reliability, fairness, and legality (Peterson, 1995).

Answering questions such as the following can assist in determining whether the data sources meet these tests:

- Are the data the responsibility of the superintendent?
- Do the data reflect responsibilities included in the superintendent's job description?
- Are the data linked to student progress, leadership, or other key responsibilities reflected in the performance standards?
- Are the data of primary importance in considering the quality of the superintendent's performance?
- Are better data available on the same performance responsibility?
- Do the data unintentionally contain any implicit biases or components with discriminatory impact?

A sound evaluation system will always be based on actual performance data collected through multiple means that are representative of the superintendent's total performance during the period covered by the performance assessment. Thus, using a more comprehensive set of data is essential and can yield a far more valuable performance assessment. Multiple data sources provide for a comprehensive and authentic "performance portrait" of the superintendent's work.

The sources of information described in table 5.1 provide the most comprehensive and accurate feedback on superintendent performance.

Table 5.1.   Data Sources for Documenting Superintendent Performance

Data Source	Description
Goal Setting and Student Progress	Superintendents have a definite impact on student progress. They set goals for improving student progress based on appropriate progress measures as part of the strategic planning process.
Document Review	Numerous documents, which are developed in the normal course of events, can be considered as part of the evaluation data collection process.
Client Surveys	Staff and/or selected community members can be insightful for assessing perceptions of clients.
Self-Assessment	Systematic self-reflection and self-assessment can be valuable in the evaluation process, particularly for assisting the superintendent in monitoring achievement and preparing for a more formal evaluation.

HOW CAN THE VARIOUS INFORMATION SOURCES BE INTEGRATED?

Goal Setting and Student Progress

If student learning is the stated objective of schooling and if superintendent evaluation is to be linked to student progress and success (see, for example, Mendro, 1998; Stronge and Tucker, 2000; Wright, Horn, and Sanders, 1997), then it appears reasonable to consider student progress when evaluating superintendents. When student progress measures are used in the evaluation of superintendents, they must conform to professional standards of practice (Joint Committee on Standards for Educational Evaluation, 2009).

There are numerous pitfalls in the inappropriate and uninformed use of assessment data for evaluation of any sort, particularly for use in personnel evaluation. It is important to maximize the benefits and minimize the liabilities in the connection of student progress and superintendent effectiveness.

School superintendents are the chief school administrators and the leaders of school districts across the nation. The inclusion of "improving student progress" as a mandatory standard of superintendent performance highlights the critical role of educational leaders in curriculum planning/development, instructional leadership, and, ultimately, student progress.

One method to employ in measuring student progress or other worthy goals is the establishment of annual performance goals. These performance goals should be aimed at desirable, yet realistic, outcomes that are congruent with the school district's needs and/or concerns.

Goals can also serve as a way to include student progress measures as one of a collection of multiple data sources. In this way, goals can serve to address a problem we presented in chapter 4 by ensuring a more fair and meaningful way to evaluate superintendents in an area where impact may be indirect (Schneider, 2019). Once established, the goals can be reviewed and adjusted as necessary.

With the use of performance goals, the superintendent typically reports progress on achieving the goals at regular intervals throughout the evaluation process. Indicators of goal attainment include documentation via the superintendent's oral and written reports as well as other evidence that can shed light on progress.

Worthy goals can be developed and documented in diverse areas such as:

- Planning and completing a building program
- Implementing a community relations effort
- Preparing for a bond referendum
- Documenting fiscal management
- Coordinating curriculum development
- Leading the educational system to increased student progress

It is important to note, especially if actual measures of student progress are to be included, that contextual issues beyond the superintendent's control can influence the realization of desired goals. For instance, there are circumstances when the superintendent (or any educator for that matter) does everything possible to enhance student learning, but conditions beyond her or his control prevent maximum benefits for students. Thus, for goals related to student learning, in addition to using multiple measures/data sources, consideration should be given to issues such as student mobility, economic influences on student success, student absenteeism, and other such variables.

Typically, a superintendent and board will jointly establish annual goals focused on improving student achievement, organizational effectiveness, or other worthy endeavors as part of the strategic planning process. Two formats are provided in Appendix C (Superintendent Annual Performance Goals) for developing and assessing annual goals. The goals and the goal fulfillment often are considered to be a primary data source in the superintendent evaluation system.

Document Review

Another important source for obtaining documentation of a superintendent's performance is analysis of artifacts (i.e., the collection of written records and documents produced under the superintendent's auspices as a part of her or his job responsibilities). Artifacts for a superintendent, for example, might include school board meeting minutes, publications written, PowerPoint notes from presentations, agendas from meetings led, record of individuals mentored, and a highlights video from press conferences.

A portfolio is a more formal collection of documents—or artifacts—that are useful for demonstrating the performance of the superintendent. Portfolio evaluation involves the systematic collection of data concerning the fulfillment of the duties or responsibilities of the superintendent organized by domains.

Some examples of items that may be included in the domain of communications and community relations are newspaper clippings, programs from various events and functions attended, or professional activities/publications. The portfolio provides a forum for dialogue on the full scope of responsibilities for the superintendent's job and provides additional information that may not have been available in any other form.

Client Surveys

In virtually every school district in America, school board members typically receive feedback, often unsolicited, regarding particular programs, events, and efforts of the superintendent and her or his staff. The feedback can come from a telephone call, a casual conversation in the grocery store, or a variety of other informal venues.

In the absence of a more systematic method for collecting perceptions of staff and community members, these anecdotal comments form the basis of the board's collective opinion of the superintendent's acceptance and performance as perceived by the school community. In essence, applying client feedback to superintendent performance—albeit informally—is common practice.

In recent years there has been a growing movement for educators to adopt 360-degree assessment principles employed in business and industry, with all segments of the school community having an opportunity to provide feedback data for the evaluation process (see, for example, Manatt, 2000). This client-centered feedback process can provide an avenue for both the superintendent and the board to receive systematic and representative feedback regarding performance.

If staff or community perceptions are to be factored into the superintendent's performance evaluation—and they invariably will—then a fairer and
more productive approach is to create a formal outlet for receiving that feedback and ensuring the feedback considered is a representative sampling of the
entire community, not just the most vocal segments. A key consideration in
collecting data using client surveys is cost.

However, the real challenge is to collect survey data so that it meets
the tests of logic, reliability, and fairness. Staff and community surveys of
a superintendent's various constituents have the potential to provide data
that meet the tests if they are well conceived, properly administered, and
interpreted fairly. At the survey conception stage, this includes avoiding or
eliminating questions that contain an unconscious bias and questions that may
contain an unintentional discriminatory component.

Unfortunately, superintendents report being evaluated on personality criteria over results-based criteria (Mayo and McCartney, 2004). Surveys with
questions that focus on the superintendent's personality traits are ripe with
potential for bias, whereas, questions that focus on superintendent actions that
are directly tied to district goals and values are less likely to produce biased
or discriminatory results.

At the interpretation stage, board member training on survey interpretation
and unconscious bias identification can serve to improve process reliability
and fairness. Additionally, while surveys can provide an important perspective on the superintendent's performance, they should be used as only one
component in the evaluation system if they are to be employed.

Tables 5.2 and 5.3 illustrate how a survey might be designed. Appendix D
provides actual sample surveys that can serve as prototypes for developing
constituent feedback forms.

Table 5.2.   Superintendent's Staff Survey Sample Items

Check One: I am __ a teacher __ an administrator __ a classified employee __ other

Superintendent's Name	School District	School Year

Directions: Read the statements about the superintendent. Select the response that
best describes your perception and mark each statement in the appropriate column.
Comments can be added in the space after the item.

The Superintendent . . .

	AGREE	DISAGREE	CANNOT JUDGE
1. Uses effective communication skills.	☐	☐	☐
2. Involves staff members in identifying and meeting school district goals.	☐	☐	☐

Table 5.3.   Superintendent's Community Survey Sample Items

The Superintendent . . .	AGREE	DISAGREE	CANNOT JUDGE
1. Uses effective communication skills.	☐	☐	☐
2. Involves parents and community members in identifying and meeting school division goals.	☐	☐	☐
3. Communicates a clear vision for the school division.	☐	☐	☐

Superintendent Self-Evaluation

The process of self-evaluation encourages the superintendent to reflect on personal experience and is closely linked to the goal-setting process. It also provides a structure for considering future goals and determining strategies for achievement.

The self-assessment process is also useful in promoting the superintendent's professional development. Data from self-evaluation may not be objective enough to use in evaluating the superintendent for summative purposes; however, a regular self-evaluation may be very useful in generating dialogue about revealed discrepancies.

Self-assessment can provide a candid preliminary evaluation that the employee may use to determine areas in which improvement is needed. It should be noted that many studies of self-evaluation have revealed that individual educators (as well as other employees) tend to perceive their performance a bit more generously than do their clients. With a basis for comparing her or his perceptions with those of others and interpreting any differences revealed by the comparison, the superintendent would be best prepared if she or he spent time assessing major accomplishments, strengths and weaknesses, reasons for disappointing results, and proposed changes in goals or objectives for the remainder of the current appraisal period or for the next one.

Table 5.4 provides an illustration of a portion of self-evaluation, and Appendix E provides a complete self-evaluation form.

Table 5.4. Superintendent Self-Assessment

DIRECTIONS This form may be used by superintendents in the ongoing
self-assessment process. Additionally, it may be well suited for use by
superintendents and board members in the interim review or formative
evaluation process. Board members may use this form to maintain records
throughout the evaluation cycle in preparation for the summative evaluation.
Thus, this form serves as a running record for documenting performance of the
superintendent from all pertinent data sources. This form should be discussed
during evaluation conferences. Place a check in the box when evidence of a
performance standard is observed/collected. Make notes in the space provided.

Domain G: Policy and Governance *Performance Standards* G-1. The Superintendent works with the School Board to develop and implement policies that define organizational expectations.	Evidence Noted

Comments

_____
_____
_____
_____
_____

HOW IS A SCORING RUBRIC USED, AND HOW IS IT HELPFUL IN JUDGING THE SUPERINTENDENT'S EFFECTIVENESS?

As described in chapter 4, the domains, job standards, and performance indicators provide a description of well-defined superintendent expectations. After collecting information gathered through goal setting, student performance
measures, client surveys, portfolio review, and other appropriate information
sources, the evidence needs to be synthesized in order to arrive at a meaningful judgment regarding performance.

One tool that can prove most helpful in making evaluation decisions—
whether for formative or summative purposes—is a rating scale, or rubric,
against which performance can be assessed. Rating scales can be designed
simply as a dichotomous scale (e.g., acceptable versus unacceptable, meets
expectations versus does not meet expectations).

However, a more beneficial approach—especially if growth and continuous improvement are key considerations—is a three- or four-point scale that offers opportunities to explain and justify performance ratings. One such example would be the four-point rating scale as illustrated in table 5.5.

Table 5.5.   Definitions of Terms in Rating Scale

Rating	Definition
Level 4: Exceeds Criteria	Performance affects students, staff, and programs in the school division in a positive manner. For performance to be rated in this category, the performance must consistently exceed the expectations set forth in the performance standards and the board should cite specific examples in a narrative format.
Level 3: Performance Meets Criteria	Performance that consistently meets expectations resulting in quality work in the accomplishment of the job performance standards identified for the superintendent. This is the acceptable performance level that is expected.
Level 2: Performance Requires Improvement	Performance that does not meet standards and requires improvement to produce desired results (i.e., to meet criteria). The board should cite specific evidence in a narrative format (i.e., describe examples of specific behaviors on the part of the superintendent that illustrate the deficiency).
Level I: Performance Is Unsatisfactory	Unacceptable performance that requires significant improvement to justify continued employment. The board should cite specific evidence in a narrative format (e.g., offering objectively written descriptions of the superintendent's behavior). The individual board member does not have enough information to rate performance on an identified standard. (See note below.)

Note: The rating Cannot Judge would be used only when an individual board member lacks sufficient information to make a fair or accurate assessment of the superintendent's performance on a specific job standard. However, in the final evaluation, the board would confer and agree on a rating drawn from the review of evidence by the entire board.

Note: An explanation of three- and four-level rating scales appears in Appendix F. In this example of a rating scale, four distinct ratings are available for use in assessing the superintendent's performance. The four-point scale enables the board to acknowledge outstanding work quality and to provide useful feedback for work that is judged to be in need of improvement.

Ratings typically are applied to individual performance standards but not to performance indicators. Additionally, ratings can be applied to the domains to provide a more global assessment of performance. Figure 5.1 illustrates how the ratings would be applied in a final evaluation, and Appendix F defines each rating. Appendices G–J offer several sample summative evaluation formats done in both the three-level rating scale and the four-level rating scale.

Superintendent's Name _____

Evaluator _____

Academic/Fiscal Year _____

<u>DIRECTIONS</u>

To be completed by the School Board as documentation of the superintendent's evaluation

■ **Domain: Planning and Assessment**

A-1. The superintendent effectively employs various processes for gathering, analyzing, and using data for decision making.

PERFORMANCE EXCEEDS CRITERIA	PERFORMANCE MEETS CRITERIA	PERFORMANCE REQUIRES IMPROVEMENT	PERFORMANCE IS UNSATISFACTORY	CANNOT JUDGE

Comments: _____
_____

Figure 5.1. **Sample Superintendent Performance Evaluation Format**

SUMMARY

In summary, we provided criteria for selecting appropriate information sources for documenting the superintendent's performance. In order to develop a complete picture of a superintendent's contribution to the overall success of the school system, we suggested that the board of education use multiple broad-based sources of information. The advantages of each of the recommended data sources were discussed and methods for integrating them were suggested. Finally, we proposed using a rating scale as a tool to make evaluation decisions. Examples of forms and materials related to these chapter elements are provided in the referenced appendices.

REFERENCES

Joint Committee on Standards for Educational Evaluation (A. R. Gullickson, Chair). (2009). *The personnel evaluation standards: How to assess systems for evaluating educators.* Newbury Park, CA: Corwin Press.

Manatt, R. P. (2000). Feedback at 360 degrees. *The school administrator web edition.* Available at http://www.aasa.org/publications/sa/2000_10/ Manatt.htm.

Mayo, C. R., and McCartney, G. P. (2004). School superintendents' evaluations: Effective and results-based? *ERS Spectrum*, 22(1), 19–33.

Mendro, R. L. (1998). Student achievement and school and teacher accountability. *Journal of Personnel Evaluation in Education*, 12, 257–67.

Peterson, K. D. (1995). *Teacher evaluation: A comprehensive guide to new directions and practices.* Thousand Oaks, CA: Corwin Press.

Schneider, T. L. (2019). A state-level superintendent evaluation policy analysis (Doctoral dissertation). Retrieved from ProQuest Dissertations and Theses (10977630).

Stronge, J. H., and Tucker, P. D. (2000). *Teacher evaluation and student achievement.* Washington, DC: National Education Association.

Wright, S. P., Horn, S. P., and Sanders, V. L. (1997). Teacher and classroom context effects on student achievement: Implications for teacher evaluation. *Journal of Personnel Evaluation in Education*, 11, 57–67.

Chapter Six

Implementing the Superintendent's Performance Evaluation

Designing performance standards, selecting sources of data, and creating documents and/or materials for a performance-based assessment of superintendents are critical initial steps. Equally important, however, is the actual implementation of the performance evaluation process.

In this chapter, basic guidelines and suggestions for implementing a superintendent performance evaluation system are provided. Specifically, the following questions are addressed:

- What policy should guide the performance evaluation of the superintendent?
- What procedures should be established?
- What kind of training is required to implement the performance evaluation of the superintendent?
- What type of review and monitoring of superintendent evaluation systems would prove beneficial to process effectiveness?

WHAT POLICY SHOULD GUIDE THE PERFORMANCE EVALUATION OF THE SUPERINTENDENT?

Superintendents often remind board members that their job is that of policy makers, not administrators. A board's policy manual should reflect the board's goals and objectives, philosophies, and methods or procedures for handling generic situations. The superintendent's job is to lead the school district within the guidelines set forth in board policy.

As discussed in chapter 3, state law often requires boards to establish a policy governing superintendent evaluation. However, seventeen states do not require superintendent evaluation or require boards to have a superintendent evaluation policy, ceding the entire process to local control. An additional eight states have such minimal requirements that they cede the specifics of the superintendent evaluation process to local control.

Even some of the states with more detailed superintendent evaluation policy requirements explicitly reserve some components for local control (Schneider, 2019). Whether or not state law requires it, we recommend that boards evaluate their superintendents annually.

Superintendent evaluation is an important responsibility of a school board that should be guided by policy. Policymaking is an opportunity for a board to set the direction and priorities of their school system. In the absence of policy, personal judgment of the superintendent or individual board members is substituted for clear guidelines established by the board. The result is often inconsistency or unreasonable practice driven by individual agendas or ambiguous goals.

The initiation of policy development begins with recognizing the need for written policy. An annual process as important as evaluating the superintendent creates such a need. Although superintendents have a significant voice in policy development recommendations (Kowalski, McCord, Petersen, Young, and Ellerson, 2011), board members share this responsibility, whether by law or best practice. Luckily, board recognition of the need for superintendent evaluation is high. Yet high board recognition does not lead to an effective process (Mayo and McCartney, 2004).

Policy Components

Both the superintendent and board members should review current policies related to the superintendent, including those that govern the evaluation of the superintendent or describe the responsibilities/duties of the superintendent. In the absence of such policy, it is important to initiate policy development.

Effective board policy in this area is:

- Collaboratively developed with the superintendent
- Reflective of the educational goals of the school district
- Written within the scope of the school board's authority
- Inclusive of state requirements for superintendent evaluation and congruent with relevant state laws/code
- Respectful of legal and constitutional rights and requirements, and mindful of confidentiality considerations

- Good personnel practice
- Adopted through proper board procedure
- Communicated to the person(s) it affects (McGee, 1988)

The district policy related to superintendent evaluation should reflect the *how*, *what*, *when*, *where*, and *by whom* the process of performance evaluation of the superintendent is to be implemented. Often, the implementation details, actual performance assessment documents and/or forms, and other details may be adopted as addenda or be incorporated into the procedures pursuant to the actual policy.

The policy itself should always reflect the board's intentions and beliefs concerning the goals of the process. Typical goals of a policy on superintendent evaluation include:

- Promoting professional excellence and improving the superintendent's skills
- Clarifying for the superintendent her or his role in the school system as understood by the board of education
- Clarifying the role of superintendent for all board of education members in light of her or his responsibilities, authority, and organizational expectations
- Developing a unified purpose in order to achieve high-priority goals and objectives
- Creating an opportunity for goal achievement through regular appraisal and feedback
- Enhancing organizational health by involving, developing, and strengthening the commitment of individual board members and the superintendent
- Establishing a shared accountability process that improves student progress;
- Assisting the superintendent in improving her or his effectiveness
- Enhancing communication between the board and the superintendent
- Enhancing communication with the greater school community (DiPaola and Stronge, 2001a, 2001b; National Education Policy Network of the National School Boards Association, n.d.; Peterson, 1989)

A sample district policy on superintendent evaluation can be found in Appendix K (adapted from the New Jersey School Boards Association [2018]).

WHAT PROCEDURES SHOULD BE ESTABLISHED?

The policy should also include or be accompanied by procedures that specify the "nuts and bolts" of the process. We believe that these elements should be clearly identified:

1. Evaluation System Components
   - Domains
   - Responsibilities/Standards (employee job expectations)
   - Sample Performance Indicators (typical behaviors for documentation)
   - Rating Scale
   - Behaviorally Anchored Rating Scale or Performance Rubric (provides descriptions of acceptable/unacceptable behavior for each job responsibility)

2. Data Sources (that will be used to document and assess job performance)
   - Formal Observation
   - Informal Observation
   - Student Progress/Goal Attainment
   - Client Satisfaction (e.g., survey data)
   - Artifact/Portfolio Data

3. Length of the Evaluation Cycle/Frequency of Evaluation

4. Forms/Materials Used in the Process
   - Summative Evaluation Form
   - Interim Review Form with Formative Feedback
   - Observation Checklist or Performance Review Form
   - Goal-Setting/Student Progress Form
   - Data Notebook Guidelines
   - Community Survey/Questionnaire
   - Staff Survey/Questionnaire
   - Improvement Plan Form

5. Training/Staff Development to Be Provided

6. Improvement Component for Evaluation System (must be aligned with school system policies/procedures and developed collaboratively with local policymakers):
   - Requirements for Improvement Plan
   - Plan of Action Forms
   - Reward/Sanction Plan (e.g., merit increase)
   - Staff Development Recommendations Based on Analysis of End-of-Cycle Evaluations (can be part of summative evaluation form)
   - Evaluation Report of Year—Implementation and Subsequent Revisions

Establishing Procedures

Once the board sets policy, procedures required for full implementation should be developed. Procedures outline the plan for *how* the process will be implemented. Additionally, policies link best to procedures that are:

- Relevant to the district
- Grounded in solid practice
- Enforceable
- Clear, concise, and concrete
- Taught and retaught through training
- Reviewed and revised periodically
- Followed by those responsible for implementing the policy

During the development of procedures, it is important to assess available resources, particularly the amount of time the implementation plan requires to be certain that it meets the *feasibility standard* so the plan can be put into practice. Implementation time includes the time to prepare and train all individuals who participate in the process.

Our experience is that the best designed evaluation process will fail to achieve its goals without the adequate training of all evaluators and evaluatees. Clearly, training is a critical component of the process.

The superintendent evaluation process that has been adopted will generally guide the sequence of implementation. Generally, an *implementation schedule* is developed first. For example, ordinarily the contract year will begin on July 1 and terminate the following June 30. We believe that training all participants is the logical initial step. If goal setting is an element of the process, it should be the next step.

Individual state law or code often dictates the frequency of evaluation. Table 6.1 contains a sample *implementation schedule* for a process that includes goal setting, interim review, and a summative review through an entire academic year with a June 30 deadline. In some states the process must be completed by the end of April if the board has intentions of terminating employment. In some states the process has an early spring deadline regardless of the board's intention.

A schedule with an April 30 deadline is in column two of table 6.1. This sample implementation schedule assumes a contract with the superintendent that would continue employment into the next year.

Table 6.1. Implementation Schedule

Summative by		
June 30	*April 30*	*Activity*
July	July	Provide training opportunities for all participants in the process
Prior to August 15	Prior to June 1	Board establishes annual district goals
Prior to September 1	Prior to July 1	Superintendent meets with board to set her or his annual goal(s) and suggest data or documents the Board could use in the evaluation process
Prior to November 15	Prior to October 15	Superintendent meets with board to discuss progress made on goal attainment and receives feedback on overall performance
Prior to January 31	Prior to January 1	Superintendent meets with board to discuss progress made on goal attainment and receives feedback on overall performance via an *Interim Review* document
Prior to April 15	Prior to March 15	Superintendent meets with board to discuss progress made on goal attainment and receive feedback on overall performance
Prior to June 30	Prior to April 30	Superintendent meets with board to discuss the annual *Summative Evaluation*

An implementation schedule creates a real ongoing process in which all parties know when each regular meeting is scheduled during the process and provides a procedural mechanism for formative and summative evaluation. We suggest that regular executive board meeting agendas actually reflect the evaluation sessions as agenda items.

This is critical since experience tells us that the most common course of action is to use time for other "pressing" issues. Not adhering to the implementation schedule undermines the process and creates an evaluation "event," the summative evaluation, at the end of the year.

WHAT KIND OF TRAINING IS REQUIRED TO IMPLEMENT THE PERFORMANCE EVALUATION OF THE SUPERINTENDENT?

Whenever a new superintendent evaluation process is adopted, training must be provided for board members as well as the superintendent. The absence of adequate training places board members in a frustrating, uncomfortable position; they should fully participate in the superintendent's evaluation, yet they do not have a clear understanding of their individual roles or of how to implement the process. When a disconnect between superintendent evaluation policy and actual implementation occurs, it undermines the intent and goals of the process, often resulting in judgments of performance grounded only in personal perceptions.

In both our national study of superintendent evaluation included within the first edition of this book, as well as the review of state-level superintendent evaluation policy included in chapter 3, we present state policy and local level evaluation lacking coherence with the *accuracy* standard. The accuracy standard requires valid, reliable, and systematic data free from bias. This finding indicates that neither states nor local boards have placed as much emphasis on ensuring that superintendent evaluations are accurate, in that the results are justified, well documented, and logically linked to data sources (Schneider, 2019).

Compounding this problem is a lack of training. Only ten of thirty-four states required evaluator training as part of the superintendent evaluation process (Schneider, 2019). Since school board members are not always trained adequately to complete evaluations to meet this criterion, the fairness of evaluations is a serious issue. In Alabama, a trained state evaluator actually conducts the evaluation of the superintendent for each board, but this is not common practice.

Although several state school board associations indicate that training is offered to school board members, the frequency and extent of the training varies. Since turnover in the ranks of school board members can be high, it is critically important that new members be trained adequately to evaluate superintendents.

We strongly suggest that the training program be designed to include these components for both superintendents and board members:

- Orientation/overview
- Application/implementation guidelines
- Establishment of student progress and other goals
- Collection of documents/artifacts

- Use of documents/artifacts for evaluation
- Use of student achievement data for evaluation
- Legal requirements for evaluation
- Conferencing skills

Reference to examples of inappropriate or ineffective practices of superintendent evaluation illustrate pitfalls to be avoided.

We advocate for the superintendent's and the entire board's participation in all phases of the evaluation process. Some school boards also elect to use an outside facilitator to assist with the superintendent's evaluation. If an outside facilitator is employed for this purpose, the facilitator should be trained in the process and meet with the superintendent and board jointly to clarify roles. Additionally, the superintendent's participation, cooperation, and support are critical.

After the annual performance evaluation is complete, we suggest that the board issue a statement during a public board meeting explaining the process and goals, as well as whatever action(s) the board has taken. The superintendent should be publicly commended whenever appropriate.

WHAT TYPE OF REVIEW AND MONITORING OF SUPERINTENDENT EVALUATION SYSTEMS WOULD PROVE BENEFICIAL TO PROCESS EFFECTIVENESS?

Even where superintendent evaluation systems exist at the state level, few states have a process for review, tracking benchmarks, or monitoring implementation efforts. At most, states are reviewing local policy. If such review or monitoring is not occurring at the state level, it is likely not occurring at the local level either. This oversight leaves the door open for, at best, implementation gaps and local boards conducting evaluations simply to satisfy a legal requirement, and, at worst, unfair or inaccurate evaluations that do not produce useful results and are used to make critical district leadership decisions (Schneider, 2019).

At the state level, states can pilot superintendent evaluation policy systems, and at the local level, boards can include a regular review of the superintendent evaluation process. Such review procedures helps to ensure that the intent of policy is operationalized in a substantive manner. In addition, regular review processes remind new board members of the ongoing aspects of evaluation as well as honor the board of education's role as representatives of the public.

There must be a balance of transparency in the superintendent evaluation process while still protecting the fairness of the process and general welfare of the superintendent. Having a policy and implementation review process helps provide that balance (Schneider, 2019).

SUMMARY

A board's responsibility as policy maker includes crafting a policy, regulations, and procedures for a quality performance evaluation system for all employees, including the superintendent. Once consensus is reached on the goals of the process, policy can begin to guide:

- Development and adoption of a comprehensive evaluation process
- Policies that specify details of the process
- Procedures and timelines for implementation
- Training of board members, the superintendent, and any other participant

Evaluating the performance of the superintendent is one of the most critical tasks of board members and should be undertaken with the same regard for planning and professionalism that is employed in selecting a superintendent. Quality evaluations enable superintendents to know which aspects of her or his performance the board feels are working well and which need improvement. The process helps establish priorities in goal setting for the next evaluation cycle and should include commendations for accomplishments as well as recommendations for improvement. Regular and systematic evaluation enhances communication and the relationship between the board and the superintendent.

REFERENCES

DiPaola, M. F., and Stronge, J. H. (2001a). Credible evaluation: Not yet state-of-the-art. *The School Administrator*, 58(2), 18–21.

DiPaola, M. F., and Stronge, J. H. (2001b). Superintendent evaluation in a standards-based environment: A status report from the states. *Journal of Personnel Evaluation in Education*, 15(2), 97–110.

Kowalski, T. J., McCord, R. S., Peterson, G. J., Young, I. P., and Ellerson, N. M. (2011). *The American school superintendent 2010 decennial study*. Lanham, MD: Rowman & Littlefield Education.

Mayo, C. R., and McCartney, G. P. (2004). School superintendents' evaluations: Effective and results-based? *ERS Spectrum*, 22(1), 19–33.

McGee, M. (1988). *School board evaluation: A comprehensive self-help guide.* Alexandria, VA: National School Boards Association.

National Education Policy Network of the National School Boards Association. (n.d.). *Evaluation of the superintendent.* Alexandria, VA: Author.

New Jersey School Boards Association (2018). *Sample district policy 2131 evaluation of the superintendent.* Trenton, NJ: Author.

Peterson, D. (1989). *Superintendent evaluation.* ERIC Digest Series Number EA 42. Eugene, OR: ERIC Clearinghouse on Educational Management.

Schneider, T. L. (2019). A state-level superintendent evaluation policy analysis (Doctoral dissertation). Retrieved from ProQuest Dissertations and Theses (10977630).

Chapter Seven

Where Do We Go from Here?

This era of accountability and standards-based reform has created a focus on performance-based assessment for all school professionals, including the superintendent. Unfortunately, within this high-stakes environment, local political pressures can often result in a deteriorating working relationship between the board and the superintendent.

This downwardly spiraling working relationship is too frequently expressed in terms of community dissatisfaction and conflict that, in turn, results in the election of new board members running on a platform that includes replacing the superintendent. Poor communication between the superintendent and the board leads to mistrust. Conflict results and unfortunately, reason disappears (Hoyle and Skrla, 1999).

Within this context, accountability is a double-edged sword that cuts to the heart of two critical issues: fair and unbiased evaluation of superintendent performance and superintendent job security. In this chapter, we discuss the impact of a sound superintendent evaluation system and provide some direction for action.

In particular, we address the following questions:

- What should superintendents and school boards do to adopt a state-of-the-art superintendent evaluation process?
- What are the benefits of superintendent evaluation for a school district and superintendent?
- How does a process of superintendent evaluation enhance the achievement of district goals?

WHAT SHOULD SUPERINTENDENTS AND SCHOOL BOARDS DO TO ADOPT A STATE-OF-THE-ART SUPERINTENDENT EVALUATION PROCESS?

A logical first step is to define criteria for a performance evaluation. The evaluation criteria recommended in this document may be modified or used as is by local school boards to achieve that goal. They are urged to carefully consider their state law, organizational goals, and their policy on evaluation before proceeding with a review of their evaluation system and criteria.

Policy should reflect organizational goals. Organizational goals should shape the job descriptions for all employees within the district, including the superintendent. Using job descriptions as a starting point, the evaluation criteria we offer can be used to further define the expectations of school superintendents.

Best practice and state-level superintendent evaluation policy in eight states link superintendent contractual provisions and superintendent evaluation results (Schneider, 2019). Superintendents should consider the evaluation process when negotiating initial and subsequent contracts. "The language governing evaluation in the superintendent's contract of employment can certainly serve to enhance the evaluation process" (Finkelstein, 2002, p. 2).

Since the interim and summative evaluation forms reflect a composite of individual board member's judgments, they may be more subjective, reflecting the sentiments of the individual(s) who prepares those documents. A contract provision stating that the superintendent receive a copy of all forms used during the process by individual board members will provide a more realistic reflection of board members' perceptions of superintendent performance.

In addition, those formative and summative evaluation forms are more frequently being tied to contractual provisions for superintendent compensation, bonuses, and/or merit pay (Schneider, 2019). The contract should also guarantee the right of the superintendent to respond to the evaluation in writing and make the response a permanent attachment to the summative document.

Evaluation as a Process, Not an Event

All too often superintendent evaluations are performed hurriedly at the last moment in an attempt to satisfy a legal requirement or a policy mandate, or, perhaps of even greater concern, in response to a recent incident. If the evaluation is merely an *event*, it has little, if any, impact on the professional growth of the superintendent or improvement of the school district.

Superintendent evaluation, when implemented as a continuous *process*, is a valuable tool that enhances communication, keeps the respective parties informed, and provides opportunities for mutual understanding, growth, and development. Only when board members and the superintendent engage in an ongoing process can the critical responsibility of the board to evaluate the superintendent be satisfactorily met.

Evaluation Timeline

There are several "natural" times for the board to examine its current practice and modify it by adopting a *process* of superintendent evaluation. They include:

- While planning for an evaluation process development during the last quarter of a school year in order to begin implementation of the process the following year
- Prior to the retirement/departure of a superintendent in order to reassess and refine expectations and the job description before a search for a successor begins
- While working with an interim superintendent

A superintendent should be included in the development phase in order for the board to get her or his perspective.

A suggested *implementation schedule* for evaluation is provided in chapter 6 (see table 6.1). Adopting such a schedule and placing quarterly meetings for the purpose of the evaluation on the board's regular meeting agenda is a first step in implementing this *process.*

These scheduled meetings provide time for the superintendent to apprise the board of progress made on established goal(s), as well as opportunities for the board members to provide feedback to the superintendent about her or his performance. They also facilitate an exchange of suggested documents and data sources that can contribute to the summative evaluation as the cycle concludes.

The time invested in the evaluation *process* has the potential to yield positive outcomes for all parties involved, as well as the entire school district. The schedule also creates a cycle of evaluation in which a summative evaluation at the end of the *process* provides guidance for goal setting at the beginning of the next evaluation cycle (see figure 7.1).

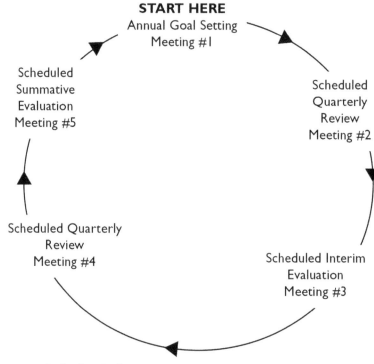

Figure 7.1. Evaluation Cycle

Implementing the Process

In using the guidelines to develop a new superintendent evaluation system:

1. Review guidelines for consistency with state and local policy for superintendent evaluation and stated purposes of evaluation, criteria, and descriptors based on job descriptions.

2. Modify evaluation criteria and descriptors to reflect local goals, job descriptions, and priorities.

3. Select information collection strategies, such as:
   • Observations
   • Client, staff, and community surveys
   • Review of documents/evidence of performance
   • Goal statements and evidence of achievement
   • Measures of student learning

- Miscellaneous sources (e.g., knowledge of professional contributions, community support)

4. Create a schedule for information collection and evaluation reports, such as:
   - Number and timing of information collection strategies
   - Calendar for administering evaluation system with deadlines for evaluation summaries

5. Establish a rating scale for judging performance, including:
   - Choice of terms
   - Definition of terms

6. Define a performance improvement process for professional educators identified as needing remedial assistance.

7. Develop necessary guidelines and forms, including:
   - Observation forms
   - Client survey forms
   - Interim formative evaluation forms
   - Summative evaluation forms
   - Improvement assistance plan

Complete guidelines for use in modifying an existing evaluation system have been provided. In using the guidelines to modify an existing superintendent evaluation system:
- Review the guidelines for consistency with state and local policy for superintendent evaluation, stated purposes of evaluation, and content of current evaluation criteria
- Make modifications to the existing evaluation system based on the requirements of applicable state laws/code, guidelines, and local needs
- Give special consideration to the integration of student learning measures in the evaluative criteria

WHAT ARE THE BENEFITS OF SUPERINTENDENT EVALUATION FOR A SCHOOL DISTRICT AND SUPERINTENDENT?

Meeting the demands for increased effectiveness of schools cannot occur without systemic change. One of the benefits of implementing an evaluation system like the one we've recommended is that it facilitates the necessary process of change. Innovative solutions are necessary for school districts to improve the achievement of all students.

This change process has created a more complex role for superintendents and board members. No longer are they able to rely on traditional ways of thinking and working a task at a time. Doing so would prevent them from envisioning the future, enticing others to participate in making that vision a reality, and creating a climate for learning.

The evaluation process can help sustain focus on systemic change initiatives. The primary goal of school districts is improving achievement for all students (Gemberling, Smith, and Villani, 2000). Implicit in this focus on continuous improvement is the need to monitor, assess, and modify.

In the evaluation process, school boards set annual goals for the district. The goals for the superintendent and all other employees must support and reflect the district goals. Think of the old and venerable adage, "What gets measured, gets done." It is through this evaluation process that the achievement of goals is monitored and "measured."

Those responsible for goal achievement are motivated to work to meet the challenges because they know their progress will be "measured." Through this accountability, the changes necessary to improve student achievement have a better chance of being sustained.

Another benefit of the process of superintendent evaluation is that it provides valuable feedback on the quality of performance. As a result, superintendents and other employees have information to plan individual professional growth and development endeavors that have direct connections to expectations of their performance.

This changes the traditional "one size fits all" professional development models and connects development activities directly to performance expectations. It makes professional growth and development a responsibility of both the superintendent and the board.

HOW DOES A PROCESS OF SUPERINTENDENT EVALUATION ENHANCE THE ACHIEVEMENT OF DISTRICT GOALS?

We hope we have made a compelling case to convince school boards and superintendents to embrace and adopt a comprehensive performance-based assessment process to evaluate chief school administrators. This collaborative process should:

- Provide clear expectations
- Use multiple data sources

- Require regular communication
- Provide useful feedback to superintendents on the quality of their performance
- Provide the constructive feedback necessary for superintendents to responsibly plan for their own professional growth and development
- Assist school board members and the superintendent in staying focused on the goals they set to help students achieve at higher levels

Superintendents should help their school boards use the resources we have provided to design and implement a sound process to assess the superintendent's performance. In the design phase, mutually agree on what outcomes you would like the process to yield.

The process must include performance criteria grounded in the real expectations of the board and community. As these evolve or change, it is important to adjust the evaluation criteria accordingly. Doing so maintains a fair, reasonable, state-of-the-art superintendent evaluation system.

The increasing expectations of and demands on the superintendent and board members often create an environment in which there never seems to be enough time to adequately address all issues. Time constraints cause board members and superintendents to struggle with proactively planning for the future.

All too often one of the issues that is shortchanged is evaluating the superintendent. We urge local school boards to recognize their responsibilities in providing a fair, comprehensive evaluation of their superintendents based on reliable and valid data. They should make the development of a performance-based evaluation process a priority.

We are confident that job satisfaction, communication, and working relationships will be enhanced when a comprehensive behavior-based performance assessment process is used to evaluate the superintendent. Such a process will help the superintendent improve her or his performance and help the school board fulfill its responsibilities. If we can use superintendent evaluation positively and proactively, we can improve the quality of our schools and, ultimately, the success of our students.

REFERENCES

DiPaola, M. F. (2010). *Evaluating the superintendent: A white paper from the American Association of School Administrators.* Alexandria, VA: AASA.

Finkelstein, B. (2002, June). Evaluating the superintendent. In *On Target* (newsletter). Trenton, NJ: New Jersey Association of School Administrators.

Gemberling, K. W., Smith, C. W., and Villani, J. S. (2000). *The keywork of school boards guidebook.* Alexandria, VA: National School Board Association.

Hoyle, J. R., and Skrla, L. (1999). The politics of superintendent evaluation. *Journal of Personnel Evaluation in Education*, 13(4), 405–19.

Schneider, T. L. (2019). A state-level superintendent evaluation policy analysis (Doctoral dissertation). Retrieved from ProQuest Dissertations and Theses (10977630).

Appendix A

American Association of School Administrators Standards and Indicators

Directions for use: These standards and indicators may be used as a guide in comparing the school district's current evaluation framework to the American Association of School Administrator's recommendations. The user may check "Y" for yes or "N" for no to note whether the indicator is part of the evaluation system.

STANDARD I: LEADERSHIP AND DISTRICT CULTURE

INDICATORS	Y	N
Formulate a written vision statement of future direction for the district		
Demonstrate an awareness of international issues affecting schools and students		
Promote academic rigor and excellence for staff and students		
Maintain personal, physical, and emotional wellness		
Empower others to reach high levels of performance		
Build self-esteem in staff and students		
Exhibit creative problem solving		
Promote and model risk taking		
Respect and encourage diversity among people and programs		
Manage time effectively		
Facilitate comparative planning between constituencies		
Conduct district school climate assessments		
Exhibit multicultural and ethnic understanding		
Promote the value of understanding and celebrating school community cultures		

STANDARD 2: POLICY AND GOVERNANCE

INDICATORS	Y	N
Describe the system of public school governance in our democracy		
Describe procedures for superintendent–board of education interpersonal and working relationships		
Formulate a district policy for external and internal programs		
Relate local policy to state and federal regulations and requirements		
Describe procedures to avoid civil and criminal liabilities		

STANDARD 3: COMMUNICATIONS AND COMMUNITY RELATIONS

INDICATORS	Y	N
Articulate district vision, mission, and priorities to the community and mass media		
Demonstrate an understanding of political theory and skills needed to build community support for district priorities		
Understand and be able to communicate with all cultural groups in the community		
Demonstrate that good judgment and actions communicate as well as words		
Develop formal and informal techniques to gain external perception of a district by means of surveys, advisory groups, and personal contact		
Communicate and project an articulate position for education		
Write and speak clearly and forcefully		
Demonstrate formal and informal listening skills		
Demonstrate group membership and leadership skills		
Identify the political forces in a community		
Identify the political context of the community environment		
Formulate strategies for passing referenda		
Persuade the community to adopt an initiative for the welfare of students		
Demonstrate conflict mediation		
Demonstrate consensus building		
Demonstrate school/community relations, school-business partnerships, and related public service activities		
Identify, track, and deal with issues		
Develop and carry out internal and external communication plans		

STANDARD 4: ORGANIZATIONAL MANAGEMENT

INDICATORS	Y	N
Define processes for gathering, analyzing, and using data for informed decision making		
Demonstrate a problem-framing process		
Define the major components of quality management		
Develop, implement, and monitor change processes to build capacities to serve clients		
Discuss legal concepts, regulations, and codes for school operations		
Describe the process of delegating responsibility for decision making		
Develop a process for maintaining accurate fiscal reporting		
Acquire, allocate, and manage human, material, and financial resources to effectively and accountably ensure successful student learning		
Use technological applications to enhance administration of business and support systems		
Demonstrate financial forecasting, planning, and cash flow management		
Perform budget planning, management, account auditing, and monitoring		
Demonstrate a grasp of practices in administering auxiliary programs, such as maintenance, facilities, food services, etc.		
Demonstrate planning and scheduling of personal time and organization work		

STANDARD 5: CURRICULUM PLANNING AND DEVELOPMENT

INDICATORS	Y	N
Develop core curriculum design and delivery systems for diverse school communities		
Describe curriculum planning/futures methods to anticipate occupational trends and their educational implication for lifelong learners		
Demonstrate an understanding of instructional taxonomies, goals, objectives, and processes		
Describe cognitive development and learning theories and their importance to the sequencing of instruction		
Demonstrate an understanding of child and adolescent growth and development		
Describe a process to create developmentally appropriate curricula and instructional practices for all children and adolescents		
Demonstrate the use of computers and other technologies in educational programming		
Conduct assessments of present and future student learning needs		
Develop a process for faculty input in continued and systematic renewal of the curriculum to ensure appropriate scope, sequence, and content		
Demonstrate an understanding of curricular alignment to ensure improved student performance and higher-order thinking		

STANDARD 6: INSTRUCTIONAL MANAGEMENT

INDICATORS	Y	N
Develop, implement, and monitor change processes to improve student learning, adult development, and climates for learning		
Demonstrate an understanding of motivation in the instructional process		
Describe classroom management theories and techniques		
Demonstrate an understanding of the development of the total student, including the physical, social, emotional, cognitive, and linguistic needs		
Formulate a plan to assess appropriate teaching methods and strategies for all learners		
Analyze available instructional resources and assign them in the most cost-effective and equitable manner to enhance student outcomes		
Describe instructional strategies that include the role of multicultural sensitivity and diverse learning styles		
Exhibit applications of computer technology connected to instructional programs		
Describe how to interpret and use testing/assessment results to improve education		
Demonstrate knowledge of research findings on the use of a variety of instructional strategies		
Describe a student achievement monitoring and reporting system		

STANDARD 7: HUMAN RESOURCES MANAGEMENT

INDICATORS	Y	N
Develop a plan to assess system and staff needs to identify areas for concentrated staff development		
Demonstrate knowledge of adult learning theory and motivation		
Evaluate the effectiveness of comprehensive staff development programming to determine its effect on professional performance		
Demonstrate use of system and staff evaluation data for personnel policy and decision making		
Monitor and improve organizational health/morale		
Demonstrate personnel management strategies		
Understand alternative benefit packages		
Assess individual and institutional sources of stress and develop methods for reducing stress (e.g., counseling, exercise programs, and diet)		
Demonstrate knowledge of personnel services and categorical programs		

STANDARD 8: VALUES AND ETHICS OF LEADERSHIP

INDICATORS	Y	N
Exhibit multicultural and ethnic understanding and sensitivity		
Describe the role of schooling in a democratic society		
Demonstrate ethical and personal integrity		
Model accepted moral and ethical standards in all interactions		
Describe a strategy to promote the value that moral and ethical practices are established and practiced in each classroom and school in a free and democratic society		
Describe a strategy to ensure that diversity of religion, ethnicity, and way of life in the district are respected		
Formulate a plan to coordinate social, health, and other community agencies for the support of each child in the district		

Appendix B

Recommended Superintendent Domains, Performance Standards, and Performance Indicators

SUPERINTENDENT DOMAINS

Domain G: Policy and Governance
Domain A: Planning and Assessment
Domain L: Instructional Leadership
Domain M: Organizational Management
Domain C: Communications and Community Relations
Domain P: Professionalism

SUPERINTENDENT EVALUATION CRITERIA: DOMAINS, PERFORMANCE STANDARDS, AND PERFORMANCE INDICATORS

Domain G: Policy and Governance

Performance Standard G-1

The Superintendent works with the school board to develop and implement policies that define organizational expectations. The superintendent . . .

- Supports and enforces all school board policies and informs all students of changes to the school board policies.
- Recommends changes to the school board when school board policies conflict with the school board's vision for education.
- Develops administrative regulations that support the application of school board policies.

- Recommends policies and procedures that protect the security and integrity of the district infrastructure and the data it contains.
- Recommends policies and procedures that protect the rights and confidentiality of staff and students.
- Maintains/improves relations between the superintendent and school board through periodic joint seminars, workshops, and training sessions.

Performance Standard G-2

The superintendent functions as the primary instructional leader for the school district, relying on support from staff as necessary when advising the school board. The superintendent . . .

- Involves staff as necessary when planning/providing recommendations to the school board.
- Demonstrates professional and personal skills, which facilitate staff involvement.
- Responds directly and factually to the school board.
- Demonstrates tact when offering recommendations.

Performance Standard G-3

The superintendent oversees the administration of the school district's day-to-day operations. The superintendent . . .

- Explores/applies operational methods, which enable the school district to apply resources in an efficient manner.
- Keeps the school board informed on needs and issues confronting school district employees.
- Informs the school board of actions that require school board involvement.
- Delegates authority and responsibility to other employees as needs/opportunities arise.

Performance Standard G-4

The superintendent works with all individuals, groups, agencies, committees, and organizations to provide and maintain schools that are safe and productive. The superintendent . . .

- Ensures safe, secure schools for all students and employees.
- Proposes improvements to school facilities, increasing public confidence and trust that schools are safe and effective learning environments.
- Uses technology to enhance professional practices and increase productivity.

Domain A: Planning and Assessment

Performance Standard A-1

The superintendent effectively employs various processes for gathering, analyzing, and using data for decision making. The superintendent . . .

- Applies current research related to effective techniques for gathering data from individuals, groups, programs, and the community.
- Uses reliable data in making decisions.
- Reviews analyses of student academic achievement through standardized test results and other academic sources.
- Provides staff with data in a collaborative effort to determine needs for improvement.
- Applies and communicates statistical findings to identify strengths and weaknesses in programs and practices in order to ensure continuous improvement.
- Plans and implements changes in programs and/or curricula based on data.
- Reviews annual analyses of district's test and subtest scores by school and discipline in order to assess school improvement and monitor improvement plans.
- Develops, monitors, and assesses district and school improvement plans.

Performance Standard A-2

The superintendent organizes the collaborative development and implementation of a district strategic plan based on analysis of data from a variety of sources. The superintendent . . .

- Provides leadership in the development of a shared vision for educational improvement and of a strategic plan to attain that vision.
- Implements strategies for the inclusion of staff and various stake holders in the planning process.
- Supports the district's mission by identifying, articulating, and planning to meet the educational needs of students, staff, and other stakeholders.
- Works collaboratively to develop long- and short-range goals and objectives consistent with the strategic plan and monitors progress in achieving long- and short-range goals and objectives.
- Provides feedback to principals on goal achievement and needs for improvement.
- Supports staff through the stages of the change process.
- Maintains stakeholders' focus on long-range mission and goals throughout the implementation process.

Performance Standard A-3

The superintendent plans, implements, supports, and assesses instructional programs that enhance teaching and student achievement of the state educational standards. The superintendent . . .

- Demonstrates a working knowledge and understanding of the state educational standards and district curricular requirements.
- Supports the development of a comprehensive curriculum utilizing goals and objectives in alignment with the state educational standards.
- Oversees the planning, implementation, evaluation, and revision of the curriculum on a systematic and ongoing basis.
- Provides resources and materials to accomplish instructional goals for all students.
- Facilitates programs/curricular changes to meet state or federal requirements.
- Monitors and assesses the effect of the programs and/or curricula on student achievement.

Performance Standard A-4

The superintendent develops plans for effective allocation of fiscal and other resources. The superintendent . . .

- Acquires, allocates, and manages district resources in compliance with all laws to ensure the effective and equitable support of all of the district's students, schools, and programs.
- Allocates resources consistent with the mission and strategic plan of the district.
- Meets and works collaboratively with the board and appropriate staff to determine priorities for budgeting and for the effective al location of space and human resources.
- Utilizes human and material resources outside the district that may support and/or enhance the achievement of goals and objectives.
- Provides adequate staffing and other resources to support technology infrastructure and integration across the school district.
- Monitors/assesses resource allocation and revises allocation plans based on implementation data.
- Oversees budget development and prepares it for school board approval.
- Implements the annual school operating budget and capital improvement plan.
- Applies financial forecasting and planning procedures that support efficient use of all school district resources.

• Maintains appropriate and accurate financial records.

Domain L: Instructional Leadership

Performance Standard L-1

The superintendent communicates a clear vision of excellence and continuous improvement consistent with the goals of the school district. The superintendent . . .

• Demonstrates personal commitment to achieving the mission of the school district.
• Articulates a shared vision to all constituencies and ensures that staff members are working in concert with the district's strategic plan.
• Informs members of the board and community of current research related to best practices in curriculum and instruction.
• Explores, disseminates, and applies knowledge and information about new or improved methods of instruction or related issues.
• Shares evaluation data and subsequent plans for continuous improvement with staff, students, and other stakeholders.
• Recognizes, encourages, and celebrates excellence among staff and students.
• Demonstrates strong motivation and high standards—models self-evaluation.
• Fosters positive morale and team spirit.

Performance Standard L-2

The superintendent oversees the alignment, coordination, and delivery of assigned programs and/or curricular areas. The superintendent . . .

• Articulates curricular goals, objectives, and frameworks to staff and other stakeholders.
• Works with staff to develop a written plan for the coordination and articulation of curricular goals.
• Works with the board, staff, and community representatives to identify needs and determine priorities regarding program delivery.
• Provides direction and support in planning and implementing activities and programs consistent with continuous improvement efforts and attainment of instructional goals.
• Monitors coordination of instructional programs with state and local standards.
• Facilitates the effective coordination and integration of district curricular and cocurricular programs.

- Reviews an annual analysis of the school vision's test and subtest scores by school and discipline in order to assess and monitor school improvement.
- Demonstrates an understanding of occupational trends and their educational implications.

Performance Standard L-3

The superintendent selects, inducts, supports, evaluates, and retains quality instructional and support personnel. The superintendent . . .

- Maintains and disseminates a current handbook of personnel policies and procedures.
- Establishes and uses selection procedures that ensure fairness and equity in selecting the best candidates.
- Makes recommendations regarding personnel decisions consistent with established policies and procedures.
- Oversees the recruitment, appointment, induction, and assignment of the most qualified personnel available.
- Establishes and implements formal and informal induction procedures to promote assistance for and acceptance of new employees.
- Sets high standards for staff performance.
- Evaluates performance of personnel consistent with district policies, provides formal and informal feedback, and maintains accurate evaluation records.
- Recommends the reappointment and/or promotion of competent, effective personnel.
- Provides support and resources for staff to improve job performance and recognizes and supports the achievements of highly effective staff members.

Performance Standard L-4

The superintendent provides staff development programs consistent with program evaluation results and school instructional improvement plans. The superintendent . . .

- Leads the development and implementation of a systematic professional development plan for individuals, including members of the board, and for the district.
- Works collaboratively with members of the staff in using student achievement data to determine relevant professional development opportunities.
- Meets with principals regularly to assess ongoing school improvement efforts.

- Evaluates the effectiveness of the professional development plan in relation to district goals.
- Encourages participation in relevant conferences, course work, and activities of professional organizations.
- Shares program evaluation results and demonstrates connection of results to ongoing staff development efforts.
- Supports staff participation in internal and external professional development opportunities as appropriate.

Performance Standard L-5

The superintendent identifies, analyzes, and resolves problems using effective problem-solving techniques. The superintendent . . .

- Identifies and addresses problems in a timely and effective manner.
- Demonstrates fairness in identifying multiple points of view around problem situations.
- Involves stakeholders in analyzing problems and developing solutions.
- Monitors implementation of problem resolutions.
- Provides shared leadership and decision-making opportunities for staff that promote a climate of collaboration and collegiality.
- Delegates responsibility appropriately to staff members.
- Maintains focus on school and district mission and goals.
- Promotes an atmosphere of mutual respect and courtesy.

Performance Standard L-6

The superintendent assesses factors affecting student achievement and serves as an agent of change for needed improvements. The superintendent . . .

- Makes appropriate changes in the curriculum and scheduling.
- Optimizes available physical resources.
- Adjusts placement of students.
- Adjusts personnel assignments.
- Provides appropriate training for instructional personnel.

Performance Standard L-7

The superintendent ensures that curricular design, instructional strategies, and learning environments integrate appropriate technologies to maximize student learning. The superintendent . . .

- Provides equitable access for students and staff to technologies that facilitate productivity and enhance learning.
- Communicates expectations that technology will be used to increase student achievement.
- Ensures that budget priorities reflect a focus on technology as it relates to enhanced learning.
- Provides technology-rich learning experiences for all students.

Domain M: Organizational Management

Performance Standard M-1

The superintendent actively supports a safe and positive environment for students and staff. The superintendent . . .

- Facilitates the implementation of sound, research-based theories and techniques of classroom management, student discipline, and school safety to ensure a safe, orderly environment conducive to teaching and learning.
- Clearly communicates expectations regarding behavior to students, staff, parents, and other members of the community.
- Clearly communicates procedures for handling disciplinary problems.
- Implements and enforces school district code of conduct and appropriate disciplinary policies and procedures in a timely and consistent manner.
- Supports effective programs through which students develop self-discipline and conflict resolution skills.
- Calmly and effectively manages emergency situations as they occur.
- Is proactive in addressing potential problem situations.
- Consistently conveys mutual respect, concern, and high expectations to students, staff, parents, and community members.
- Recognizes students and staff for their academic, cocurricular, personal, and professional achievements.

Performance Standard M-2

The superintendent develops procedures for working with the board of education that define mutual expectations, working relationships, and strategies for formulating district policies. The superintendent . . .

- Respects the policymaking authority and responsibility of the board.
- Develops and uses a systematic means of keeping members of the board informed with complete, accurate information.

- Facilitates the delineation of superintendent and board roles and the articulation of mutual expectations.
- Recommends policy additions and/or modifications to improve student learning and district effectiveness.
- Anticipates future needs and demonstrates a bias for action.
- Values group interaction and problem solving.
- Expresses opinions on policy issues directly to the board.
- Supports and implements policy established by the board.

Performance Standard M-3

The superintendent effectively manages human, material, and financial resources to ensure student progress and to comply with legal man dates. The superintendent . . .

- Complies with federal, state, and local statutes, regulations, policies, and procedures.
- Collaboratively plans and prepares a fiscally responsible budget to support the organization's mission and goals.
- Demonstrates effectiveness in obtaining necessary resources.
- Establishes and uses accepted procedures for receiving and disbursing funds.
- Ensures that expenditures are within limits approved by the board.
- Implements appropriate management techniques and group processes to define roles, delegate activities and responsibilities, and determine accountability for goal attainment.
- Prepares and implements short- and long-range plans for facilities and sites.
- Ensures proper maintenance and repair of district property and equipment.
- Monitors any construction, renovation, or demolition of district buildings.
- Regularly reports to the board on the financial condition of the district.
- Monitors the efficient use of resources.
- Works with staff to establish an effective schedule for use of shared resources.
- Ensures the maintenance of accurate personnel records.

Performance Standard M-4

The superintendent demonstrates effective organizational skills to achieve school, community, and district goals. The superintendent . . .

- Demonstrates and communicates a working knowledge and under standing of school district policies and procedures.
- Ensures compliance and follow-through regarding policies and procedures.
- Uses time to the best advantage, manages scheduling effectively, and follows tasks to completion.
- Employs appropriate technologies to communicate, manage schedules and resources, assess performance, and enhance learning.
- Performs duties in an accurate and timely manner.
- Maintains appropriate and accurate records.
- Efficiently and appropriately prioritizes and addresses multiple is sues and projects.
- Systematically evaluates progress on achieving established goals.
- Keeps the board, staff, and community apprised of progress in achieving the district's goals.

Performance Standard M-5

The superintendent implements sound personnel procedures in recruiting, employing, and retaining the best qualified and most competent teachers, administrators, and other personnel. The superintendent . . .

- Knows and follows proper procedures for staffing.
- Recruits and assigns the best available personnel in terms of personal and professional competence.
- Establishes and uses selection procedures that ensure fairness and equity in selecting the best candidates for employment and promotions.
- Establishes and implements formal and informal induction procedures for new employees.
- Assigns and transfers employees as the needs of the school district dictate and reports such information to the school board.

Performance Standard M-6

The superintendent provides staff development for all categories of personnel consistent with individual needs, program evaluation results, and instructional improvement plans. The superintendent . . .

- Oversees the planning and evaluation of the staff development program.
- Works collaboratively with members of the staff in using student achievement data to identify relevant professional development needs.
- Encourages and supports employee participation in appropriate internal and external development opportunities.

- Maintains an emphasis on technological fluency and provides staff development opportunities to support high expectations.

Performance Standard M-7

The superintendent plans and implements a systematic employee performance evaluation system. The superintendent . . .

- Establishes a fair and meaningful employee evaluation system that promotes high expectations of all staff.
- Establishes evaluation procedures that assess demonstrated growth in achieving technology standards.
- Provides training for all administrative and supervisory personnel in the evaluation and documentation of teacher and administrative performance that includes student achievement as a criterion.
- Provides for positive recognition of identified strengths and accomplishments.
- Provides assistance to employees requiring remediation.
- Provides oversight in the identification of strengths and weaknesses of employees, formal and informal feedback, and dismissal of ineffective employees.
- Provides an annual report to the school board summarizing the results of employee evaluations.

Domain C: Communications and Community Relations

Performance Standard C-1

The superintendent promotes effective communication and interpersonal relations within the school district. The superintendent . . .

- Promotes a climate of trust and teamwork within the district.
- Facilitates constructive and timely communication.
- Initiates communication and facilitates cooperation among staff regarding curriculum or program initiatives.
- Establishes a culture that encourages responsible risk taking while requiring accountability for results.
- Models professionally appropriate communication skills, interpersonal relations, and conflict mediation.
- Maintains visibility and accessibility to staff.
- Solicits staff input to discuss issues and goals and to promote effective decision making.

- Establishes and maintains a collaborative relationship with staff members in promoting the district's mission and in communicating expectations.

Performance Standard C-2

The superintendent establishes and maintains effective channels of communication with board members and between the schools and com munity, strengthening support of constituencies and building coalitions. The superintendent . . .

- Accepts responsibility for maintaining communication between the board and district personnel.
- Anticipates, analyzes, and discusses emerging educational/district issues with the board on a regular basis.
- Systematically provides accurate, relevant information to the board to facilitate decision making.
- Establishes, maintains, and evaluates a planned, two-way system of communication with community constituencies.
- Communicates school and district goals, objectives, and expectations to stakeholders.
- Is politically astute and demonstrates the skills necessary to build community support for district goals and priorities.
- Works cooperatively with representatives of the news media.
- Establishes partnerships with public and private agencies to enhance the district's ability to serve students and other constituents.
- Uses acceptable written and oral language.

Performance Standard C-3

The superintendent works collaboratively with staff, families, and community members to secure resources and to support the success of a diverse student population. The superintendent . . .

- Is responsive to the conditions and dynamics of the diversity within the school community.
- Treats people with respect.
- Models and promotes multicultural awareness, gender sensitivity, and the appreciation of diversity in the community.
- Is knowledgeable about laws regarding individual and group rights and responsibilities and scrupulously avoids actions that might violate them.
- Collaborates with staff, families, and community leaders and responds to identified needs of individual students and groups of students.

- Promotes the value of understanding and celebrating school/ community cultures.

Performance Standard C-4

The superintendent creates an atmosphere of trust and mutual respect with staff and community. The superintendent . . .

- Unites people toward a common goal.
- Fosters an environment conducive to the teaching and learning process.
- Promotes collaboration and collegiality among the staff.
- Treats all personnel fairly without favoritism or discrimination while demanding high-performance standards.

Domain P: Professionalism

Performance Standard P-1

The superintendent models professional, moral, and ethical standards as well as personal integrity in all interactions. The superintendent . . .

- Understands and models appropriate value systems, ethics, and moral leadership.
- Promotes the establishment and application of moral and ethical practices in each school and classroom.
- Relates to board members, staff, and others in an ethical and professional manner.
- Maintains the physical and emotional wellness necessary to meet the responsibilities of the position.
- Serves as an articulate spokesperson for the school district and rep resents the district favorably at the local, state, and national levels.
- Resolves concerns and problems in an appropriate manner.
- Respects and maintains confidentiality and assumes responsibility for personal actions and those of subordinates.
- Maintains a professional demeanor and appearance appropriate to responsibilities.
- Demonstrates good character and integrity.

Performance Standard P-2

The superintendent works in a collegial and collaborative manner with school personnel and the community to promote and support the mission and goals of the school district. The superintendent . . .

- Demonstrates flexibility and a collaborative attitude in supporting professionals/other staff/work teams.
- Supports the district and advances its mission/goals.
- Establishes and supports a district culture that encourages collaboration and teamwork in achieving goals.
- Maintains effective working relationships with other administrators and staff.
- Shares ideas and information and considers the interests and needs of staff members and community stakeholders in promoting and supporting district goals and services.

Performance Standard P-3

The superintendent takes responsibility for and participates in a meaningful and continuous process of professional development that results in the enhancement of student learning. The superintendent . . .

- Participates in professional growth activities, including conferences, workshops, course work, and/or membership in professional organizations at the district, state, and/or national levels.
- Evaluates and identifies areas of personal strength and weakness related to providing district leadership.
- Sets goals for improvement of skills and professional performance.
- Maintains a high level of personal knowledge regarding new developments and techniques, including technology, and shares the in formation with appropriate staff.
- Comprehends and applies current research on educational issues, trends, and practices.
- Networks with colleagues to share knowledge about effective educational practices and to improve and enhance administrative knowledge, skills, and organizational success.
- Maintains proper licensure and certification.

Performance Standard P-4

The superintendent provides service to the profession, the district, and the community. The superintendent . . .

- Serves on district, state, and/or national committees and maintains an active role in professional organizations.
- Contributes to and supports the development of the profession by serving as an instructor, mentor, coach, presenter, researcher, or supervisor.

- Organizes, facilitates, and presents at local, state, and/or national conferences.
- Supports and participates in efforts to align district goals and activities with community endeavors.

Appendix C

Superintendent Annual
Performance Goals

■ SAMPLE I ■

Superintendent Annual Performance Goals

Superintendent _____ Evaluator_____

Academic/Fiscal Year _____ School District _____

Goal/Objective:						
Indicators of Success	Superintendent's Assessment					Board Assessment
	Achieved	Partially Achieved	Not Achieved	Agree	Disagree	Comments

SAMPLE II (2 pages)

Superintendent Annual Performance Goals

Superintendent:

Academic Year:

Focus *[The area/topic to be addressed (e.g., student learning, school safety)]*

Baseline Data *[status at beginning of year]*

Goal Statement *[desired result(s)]*

Board Members' Signatures/Date

■ **SAMPLE II (2 Pages)** ■

Superintendent Annual Performance Goals

Timeline for Goal Achievement *[quarterly progress report]*

Quarter	Benchmarks (target expectation by given date)	Activities	Interim Results (achieved results by given date)	Board Member Initials
October 1				
January 1				
April 1				
June 30				

Appendix D

Staff and Community Surveys

Suggestions for use: After receiving the surveys back, make a tally chart by question of the responses. Look for areas where stakeholders are recognizing strengths and identifying weaknesses. The survey results may serve as one of the multiple forms of evidence of a superintendent's effectiveness as the results demonstrate how the stakeholders perceive the superintendent.

Appendix D

■ Superintendent ■

Community Survey

Check One: I am a ___ parent ___ community member ___ public official ___ other

_____ _____ _____
Superintendent's Name   School District   School Year

Directions: Read the statements about the superintendent. Select the response that best describes your perception and mark each statement in the appropriate column. Comments can be added in the space after the item or on the back.

The Superintendent . . .

	AGREE	DISAGREE	CANNOT JUDGE
1. Uses effective communication skills	❑	❑	❑
2. Involves parents and community members in identifying and meeting school district goals	❑	❑	❑
3. Communicates a clear vision for the school district	❑	❑	❑
4. Seeks to obtain community support for school district goals	❑	❑	❑
5. Relates to all people in a courteous and professional manner	❑	❑	❑
6. Supports community activities	❑	❑	❑
7. Aligns school district goals with community needs	❑	❑	❑
8. Communicates and supports clear and consistent expectations for student behavior	❑	❑	❑
9. Is approachable and accessible to parents and other community members	❑	❑	❑
10. Applies policies and regulations in a fair and consistent manner	❑	❑	❑
11. Is a positive ambassador for the school district	❑	❑	❑
12. Handles emergency situations appropriately	❑	❑	❑
13. Is responsive to the needs of all constituencies/ cultures in our community	❑	❑	❑
14. Ensures well-maintained facilities that meet program/demographic requirements	❑	❑	❑
15. Shares student assessment data and improvement plans with parents and other community members	❑	❑	❑
16. Shares district assessment data with parents and other stakeholders	❑	❑	❑
17. Resolves problems and concerns in an appropriate manner	❑	❑	❑
18. Recognizes and encourages excellence among students and staff	❑	❑	❑
19. Ensures student/school safety	❑	❑	❑
20. Keeps me informed about school district programs and goals	❑	❑	❑

Thank you for your feedback.

■ Superintendent ■

Staff Survey

Check One: I am a ___ teacher ___ an administrator ___ a classified employee ___ other

_____   _____   _____
Superintendent's Name   School District   School Year

Directions: Read the statements about the superintendent. Select the response that best describes your perception and mark each statement in the appropriate column. Comments can be added in the space after the item.

The Superintendent ...	AGREE	DISAGREE	CANNOT JUDGE
1. Uses effective communication skills	❑	❑	❑
2. Involves staff members in identifying and meeting school district goals	❑	❑	❑
3. Communicates a clear vision for the school district	❑	❑	❑
4. Seeks to obtain staff and community support for school district goals and priorities	❑	❑	❑
5. Relates to all constituencies in a courteous and professional manner	❑	❑	❑
6. Supports school and community activities	❑	❑	❑
7. Aligns school district goals with community needs and priorities	❑	❑	❑
8. Communicates and supports clear and consistent expectations for student behavior	❑	❑	❑
9. Is approachable and accessible	❑	❑	❑
10. Applies policies and regulations in a fair and consistent manner	❑	❑	❑
11. Is a positive ambassador for the school district	❑	❑	❑
12. Handles emergency situations in a calm and appropriate manner	❑	❑	❑
13. Uses sound financial management practices	❑	❑	❑
14. Is responsive to the needs of all constituencies/ cultures in our community	❑	❑	❑
15. Ensures well-maintained facilities that meet program/demographic requirements	❑	❑	❑
16. Shares student assessment data and improvement plans with staff	❑	❑	❑
17. Delegates responsibility effectively and appropriately	❑	❑	❑
18. Provides direction and support for instruction	❑	❑	❑
19. Demonstrates a commitment to students	❑	❑	❑
20. Resolves problems and concerns in an appropriate manner	❑	❑	❑
21. Recognizes and encourages excellence among students and staff	❑	❑	❑
22. Ensures student/school safety	❑	❑	❑
23. Encourages teamwork and collaboration	❑	❑	❑

	AGREE	DISAGREE	CANNOT JUDGE
24. Conducts meetings that are meaningful and productive	❏	❏	❏
25. Shares district assessment data and improvement plans with staff	❏	❏	❏
26. Is approachable and accessible to staff	❏	❏	❏
27. Maintains high standards of ethics, honesty, and integrity	❏	❏	❏
28. Encourages and supports professional growth and development that meet district needs and priorities	❏	❏	❏
29. Distributes resources equitably and efficiently	❏	❏	❏

Thank you for your feedback.

Appendix E

Self-Assessment, Performance Checklist, and Interim Review

■ **Superintendent** ■

Self-Assessment / Performance Checklist / Interim Review

Superintendent's Name _____

Evaluator _____

Academic/Fiscal Year _____

<u>Directions</u> This form may be used by superintendents in the ongoing self-assessment process. Additionally, it may be well suited for use by superintendents and board members in the interim review or formative evaluation process. Board members may use this form to maintain records throughout the evaluation cycle in preparation for the summative evaluation. Thus, this form serves as a running record for documenting performance of the superintendent from all pertinent data sources. This form should be discussed during evaluation conferences. Place a check in the box when evidence of a performance standard is observed/collected. Make notes in the space provided.

Domain G: Policy and Governance *Performance Standards*	**Evidence Noted**
G-1. The superintendent works with the school board to develop and implement policies that define organizational expectations. *Notes*	
G-2. The superintendent functions as the primary instructional leader for the school district, relying on support from staff as necessary when advising the school board. *Notes*	
G-3. The superintendent oversees the administration of the school district's day-to-day operations. *Notes*	
G-4. The superintendent works with all individuals, groups, agencies, committees, and organizations to provide and maintain schools that are safe and productive. *Notes*	

Additional Notes

_____
_____
_____

Domain A: Planning and Assessment *Performance Standards*	Evidence Noted
A-1. The superintendent effectively employs various processes for gathering, analyzing, and using data for decision making. *Notes*	
A-2. The superintendent organizes the collaborative development implementation of a district strategic plan based on analysis of data from a variety of sources. *Notes*	
A-3. The superintendent plans, implements, supports, and assesses instructional programs that enhance teaching and student achievement of the state educational standards. *Notes*	
A-4. The superintendent develops plans for effective allocation of fiscal and other resources. *Notes*	

Domain L: Instructional Leadership *Performance Standards*	Evidence Noted
L-1. The superintendent communicates a clear vision of excellence and continuous improvement consistent with the goals of the school district. *Notes*	
L-2. The superintendent oversees the alignment, coordination, and delivery of assigned programs and/or curricular areas. *Notes*	
L-3. The superintendent selects, inducts, supports, evaluates, and retains quality instructional and support personnel. *Notes*	
L-4. The superintendent provides staff development programs consistent with program evaluation results and school instructional improvement plans. *Notes*	
L-5. The superintendent identifies, analyzes, and resolves problems using effective problem-solving techniques. *Notes*	
L-6. The superintendent assesses factors affecting student achievement and serves as an agent of change for needed improvements. *Notes*	

Additional Notes

_____

_____

Domain M: Organizational Management *Performance Standards*	Evidence Noted
M-1. The superintendent actively supports a safe and positive environment for students and staff. *Notes*	
M-2. The superintendent develops procedures for working with the board of education that define mutual expectations, working relationships, and strategies for formulating district policies. *Notes*	
M-3. The superintendent effectively manages human, material, and financial resources to ensure student learning and to comply with legal mandates. *Notes*	
M-4. The superintendent demonstrates effective organizational skills to achieve school, community, and district goals. *Notes*	
M-5. The superintendent implements sound personnel procedures in recruiting, employing, and retaining the best qualified and most competent teachers, administrators, and other personnel. *Notes*	
M-6. The superintendent provides staff development for all categories of personnel consistent with individual needs, program evaluation results, and instructional improvement plans. *Notes*	
M-7. The superintendent plans and implements a systematic employee performance evaluation system. *Notes*	

Domain C: Communications & Community Relations *Performance Standards*	Evidence Noted
C-1. The superintendent promotes effective communication and interpersonal relations within the school district. *Notes*	
C-2. The superintendent establishes and maintains effective channels of communication with board members and between the schools and community, strengthening support of constituencies and building coalitions. *Notes*	
C-3. The superintendent works collaboratively with staff, families, and community members to secure resources and to support the success of a diverse student population. *Notes*	
C-4. The superintendent creates an atmosphere of trust and mutual respect with staff and community. *Notes*	

Domain P: Professionalism *Performance Standards*	Evidence Noted
P-1. The superintendent models professional, moral, and ethical standards as well as personal integrity in all interactions. *Notes*	
P-2. The superintendent works in a collegial and collaborative manner with school personnel and the community to promote and support the mission and goals of the school district. *Notes*	
P-3. The superintendent takes responsibility for and participates in a meaningful and continuous process of professional development that results in the enhancement of student learning. *Notes*	
P-4. The superintendent provides service to the profession, the district, and the community. *Notes*	

Summary

Strengths

Areas for Improvement

_____ Recommend continued employment in current position
_____ Requires action/intervention plan for improvement [ATTACH PLAN]
_____ Recommend continued employment but not in current position
_____ Recommend dismissal

Signatures:

_____   _____
Superintendent/Date   Evaluator/Date

EMPLOYEE SIGNATURE ACKNOWLEDGES RECEIPT OF THIS FORM. WRITTEN COMMENTS MAY BE ATTACHED.
COMMENTS ATTACHED: __YES __ NO

Appendix F

Superintendent
Summative Evaluation

EXPLANATION OF RATING SCALE

There are two major considerations in assessing job performance during summative evaluation: the actual standards and how well they are performed. The domains, performance standards, and performance indicators provide a description of well-defined superintendent expectations. Appendix B provides guidelines for assessment. After collecting information gathered through goal achievement, observation, student performance measures, review of artifacts, and other appropriate sources, the Board would use a three- or four-point rating scale to evaluate performance of superintendent standards. The rating scale provides a description of different levels of how well the duties (i.e., standards) are performed on a continuum from "exceeds expectations" to "unsatisfactory." The use of the four-level rating scale enables School Board members to acknowledge effective performance (i.e., "exceeds expectations" and "meets expectations") and provides two levels of feedback for superintendents not meeting expectations (i.e., "needs improvement" and "unsatisfactory"). The three-level rating scale enables Board members to acknowledge effective performance (i.e., "exceeds expectations" and "meets expectations") and provides one level of feedback for superintendents not meeting expectations ("has not met expectations"). Ratings are applied either to domains or individual standards, but not to performance indicators. The following sections define the various rating levels, provide detailed information on the performance of standards for improvement purposes, and describe the decision-making process for assessing performance.

4-Level Rating Scale

Rating	Definition
Exceeds Criteria / Expectations	The superintendent surpasses required standards, consistently producing exemplary work that optimizes district goals and priorities.
Meets Criteria / Expectations	The performance of the superintendent consistently fulfills standards resulting in quality work that affects district goals and priorities in a positive manner. *This rating is a high performance standard and is expected of all superintendents.*
Needs Improvement / Requires Assistance	The superintendent inconsistently meets standards resulting in less than quality work performance where district goals and priorities need improvement.
Unsatisfactory	The superintendent does not adequately fulfill responsibilities, resulting in inferior work performance and negatively influencing district goals and priorities.

3-Level Rating Scale

Rating	Definition
Exceeds Criteria / Expectations	The superintendent surpasses required standards, consistently producing exemplary work that optimizes district goals and priorities.
Meets Criteria / Expectations	The performance of the superintendent consistently fulfills standards resulting in quality work that affects district goals and priorities in a positive manner. *This rating is a high performance standard and is expected of all superintendents.*
Has Not Met Expectations	The superintendent inconsistently or has not adequately met the standards, resulting in less than quality work.

Appendix G

Sample
Summative Evaluation Form I

148 *Appendix G*

■ 4-level rating scale (9 pages) ■

Superintendent Summative Evaluation

Superintendent's Name _____

Evaluator _____

Academic/Fiscal Year _____

<u>Directions</u>

To be completed by the School Board as documentation of the superintendent's evaluation.

■ Domain G: Policy and Governance

Performance Standards

G-1.   The superintendent works with the school board to develop and implement policies that define organizational expectations.

PERFORMANCE EXCEEDS CRITERIA	PERFORMANCE MEETS CRITERIA	PERFORMANCE REQUIRES IMPROVEMENT	PERFORMANCE IS UNSATISFACTORY	CANNOT JUDGE

Comments:

_____

_____

G-2.   The superintendent functions as the primary instructional leader for the school district, relying on support from staff as necessary when advising the school board.

PERFORMANCE EXCEEDS CRITERIA	PERFORMANCE MEETS CRITERIA	PERFORMANCE REQUIRES IMPROVEMENT	PERFORMANCE IS UNSATISFACTORY	CANNOT JUDGE

Comments:

_____

_____

G-3.   The superintendent oversees the administration of the school district's day-to-day operations.

Comments:

_____

_____

PERFORMANCE EXCEEDS CRITERIA	PERFORMANCE MEETS CRITERIA	PERFORMANCE REQUIRES IMPROVEMENT	PERFORMANCE IS UNSATISFACTORY	CANNOT JUDGE

Comments:

_____

_____

G-4. The superintendent works with all individuals, groups, agencies, committees, and organizations to provide and maintain schools that are safe and productive.

PERFORMANCE EXCEEDS CRITERIA	PERFORMANCE MEETS CRITERIA	HAS NOT MET PERFORMANCE CRITERIA	CANNOT JUDGE

Comments:

_____

_____

■ Domain A: Planning and Assessment

Performance Standards

A-1. The superintendent effectively employs various processes for gathering, analyzing, and using data for decision making.

PERFORMANCE EXCEEDS CRITERIA	PERFORMANCE MEETS CRITERIA	HAS NOT MET PERFORMANCE CRITERIA	CANNOT JUDGE

Comments:

_____

_____

A-2. The superintendent organizes the collaborative development and implementation of a district strategic plan based on analysis of data from a variety of sources.

PERFORMANCE EXCEEDS CRITERIA	PERFORMANCE MEETS CRITERIA	HAS NOT MET PERFORMANCE CRITERIA	CANNOT JUDGE

Comments:

_____

_____

A-3. The superintendent plans, implements, supports, and assesses instructional programs that enhance teaching and student achievement of the state educational standards.

PERFORMANCE EXCEEDS CRITERIA	PERFORMANCE MEETS CRITERIA	HAS NOT MET PERFORMANCE CRITERIA	CANNOT JUDGE

Comments:

_____

_____

A-4. The superintendent develops plans for effective allocation of fiscal and other resources.

PERFORMANCE EXCEEDS CRITERIA	PERFORMANCE MEETS CRITERIA	HAS NOT MET PERFORMANCE CRITERIA	CANNOT JUDGE

Comments:

■ Domain L: Instructional Leadership

Performance Standards

L-1. The superintendent communicates a clear vision of excellence and continuous improvement consistent with the goals of the school district.

PERFORMANCE EXCEEDS CRITERIA	PERFORMANCE MEETS CRITERIA	HAS NOT MET PERFORMANCE CRITERIA	CANNOT JUDGE

Comments:

L-2. The superintendent oversees the alignment, coordination, and delivery of assigned programs and/or curricular areas.

PERFORMANCE EXCEEDS CRITERIA	PERFORMANCE MEETS CRITERIA	HAS NOT MET PERFORMANCE CRITERIA	CANNOT JUDGE

Comments:

L-3. The superintendent selects, inducts, supports, evaluates, and retains quality instructional and support personnel.

PERFORMANCE EXCEEDS CRITERIA	PERFORMANCE MEETS CRITERIA	HAS NOT MET PERFORMANCE CRITERIA	CANNOT JUDGE

Comments:

L-4.   The superintendent provides staff development programs consistent with the program evaluation results and school instructional improvement plans.

PERFORMANCE EXCEEDS CRITERIA	PERFORMANCE MEETS CRITERIA	HAS NOT MET PERFORMANCE CRITERIA	CANNOT JUDGE

Comments:
_____
_____

L-5.   The superintendent identifies, analyzes, and resolves problems using effective problem-solving techniques.

PERFORMANCE EXCEEDS CRITERIA	PERFORMANCE MEETS CRITERIA	HAS NOT MET PERFORMANCE CRITERIA	CANNOT JUDGE

Comments:
_____
_____

L-6.   The superintendent assesses factors affecting student achievement and serves as an agent of change for needed improvements.

PERFORMANCE EXCEEDS CRITERIA	PERFORMANCE MEETS CRITERIA	HAS NOT MET PERFORMANCE CRITERIA	CANNOT JUDGE

Comments:
_____
_____

■ Domain M: Organizational Management

Performance Standards

M-1.   The superintendent actively supports a safe and positive environment for students and staff.

PERFORMANCE EXCEEDS CRITERIA	PERFORMANCE MEETS CRITERIA	HAS NOT MET PERFORMANCE CRITERIA	CANNOT JUDGE

Comments:
_____
_____

M-2. The superintendent develops procedures for working with the board of education that define mutual expectations, working relationships, and strategies for formulating district policies.

PERFORMANCE EXCEEDS CRITERIA	PERFORMANCE MEETS CRITERIA	HAS NOT MET PERFORMANCE CRITERIA	CANNOT JUDGE

Comments:

_____

_____

M-3. The superintendent effectively manages human, material, and financial resources to ensure student learning and to comply with legal mandates.

PERFORMANCE EXCEEDS CRITERIA	PERFORMANCE MEETS CRITERIA	HAS NOT MET PERFORMANCE CRITERIA	CANNOT JUDGE

Comments:

_____

_____

M-4. The superintendent demonstrates effective organizational skills to achieve school, community, and district goals.

PERFORMANCE EXCEEDS CRITERIA	PERFORMANCE MEETS CRITERIA	HAS NOT MET PERFORMANCE CRITERIA	CANNOT JUDGE

Comments:

_____

_____

M-5. The superintendent implements sound personnel procedures in recruiting, employing, and retaining the best qualified and most competent teachers, administrators, and other personnel.

PERFORMANCE EXCEEDS CRITERIA	PERFORMANCE MEETS CRITERIA	HAS NOT MET PERFORMANCE CRITERIA	CANNOT JUDGE

Comments:

_____

_____

M-6. The superintendent provides staff development for all categories of personnel consistent with individual needs, program evaluation results, and instructional improvement plans.

PERFORMANCE EXCEEDS CRITERIA	PERFORMANCE MEETS CRITERIA	HAS NOT MET PERFORMANCE CRITERIA	CANNOT JUDGE

Comments:

_____

_____

M-7. The superintendent plans and implements a systematic employee performance evaluation system.

PERFORMANCE EXCEEDS CRITERIA	PERFORMANCE MEETS CRITERIA	HAS NOT MET PERFORMANCE CRITERIA	CANNOT JUDGE

Comments:

_____

_____

■ Domain C: Communications and Community Relations

Performance Standards

C-1. The superintendent promotes effective communication and interpersonal relations within the school district.

PERFORMANCE EXCEEDS CRITERIA	PERFORMANCE MEETS CRITERIA	HAS NOT MET PERFORMANCE CRITERIA	CANNOT JUDGE

Comments:

_____

_____

C-2. The superintendent establishes and maintains effective channels of communication with board members and between the schools and community, strengthening support of constituencies and building coalitions.

PERFORMANCE EXCEEDS CRITERIA	PERFORMANCE MEETS CRITERIA	HAS NOT MET PERFORMANCE CRITERIA	CANNOT JUDGE

Comments:

_____

_____

C-3. The superintendent works collaboratively with staff, families, and community members to secure resources and to support the success of a diverse student population.

PERFORMANCE EXCEEDS CRITERIA	PERFORMANCE MEETS CRITERIA	HAS NOT MET PERFORMANCE CRITERIA	CANNOT JUDGE

Comments:

_____

_____

C-4. The superintendent creates an atmosphere of trust and mutual respect with staff and community.

PERFORMANCE EXCEEDS CRITERIA	PERFORMANCE MEETS CRITERIA	HAS NOT MET PERFORMANCE CRITERIA	CANNOT JUDGE

Comments:

_____

_____

■ Domain P: Professionalism

Performance Standards

P-1. The superintendent models professional, moral, and ethical standards as well as personal integrity in all interactions.

PERFORMANCE EXCEEDS CRITERIA	PERFORMANCE MEETS CRITERIA	HAS NOT MET PERFORMANCE CRITERIA	CANNOT JUDGE

Comments:

_____

_____

P-2. The superintendent works in a collegial and collaborative manner with school personnel and the community to promote and support the mission and goals of the school district.

PERFORMANCE EXCEEDS CRITERIA	PERFORMANCE MEETS CRITERIA	HAS NOT MET PERFORMANCE CRITERIA	CANNOT JUDGE

Comments:

_____

_____

P-3.   The superintendent takes responsibility for and participates in a meaningful and continuous process of professional development that results in the enhancement of student learning.

PERFORMANCE EXCEEDS CRITERIA	PERFORMANCE MEETS CRITERIA	HAS NOT MET PERFORMANCE CRITERIA	CANNOT JUDGE

Comments:

_____

_____

P-4.   The superintendent provides service to the profession, the district, and the community.

PERFORMANCE EXCEEDS CRITERIA	PERFORMANCE MEETS CRITERIA	HAS NOT MET PERFORMANCE CRITERIA	CANNOT JUDGE

Comments:

_____

_____

■ **Evaluation Summary** ■

■ **Strengths**

■ **Areas for Improvement**

Signatures:

_____   _____
Superintendent   School Board Chair

_____   _____
Date   Date

SUPERINTENDENT'S SIGNATURE ACKNOWLEDGES RECEIPT OF THIS FORM.
WRITTEN COMMENTS MAY BE ATTACHED.
COMMENTS ATTACHED: ____ YES   ____ NO

■ 3-level rating scale (9 pages) ■

Superintendent Summative Evaluation

Superintendent's Name _____
Evaluator _____
Academic/Fiscal Year _____

<u>DIRECTIONS</u>
To be completed by the School Board as documentation of the superintendent's evaluation.

■ Domain G: Policy and Governance

Performance Standards

G-1.   The superintendent works with the school board to develop and implement policies that define organizational expectations.

PERFORMANCE EXCEEDS CRITERIA	PERFORMANCE MEETS CRITERIA	HAS NOT MET PERFORMANCE CRITERIA	CANNOT JUDGE

Comments:
_____
_____

G-2.   The superintendent functions as the primary instructional leader for the school district, relying on support from staff as necessary when advising the school board.

PERFORMANCE EXCEEDS CRITERIA	PERFORMANCE MEETS CRITERIA	HAS NOT MET PERFORMANCE CRITERIA	CANNOT JUDGE

Comments:
_____
_____

G-3.   The superintendent oversees the administration of the school district's day-to-day operations.

PERFORMANCE EXCEEDS CRITERIA	PERFORMANCE MEETS CRITERIA	HAS NOT MET PERFORMANCE CRITERIA	CANNOT JUDGE

Comments:
_____
_____

G-4.   The superintendent works with all individuals, groups, agencies, committees, and organizations to provide and maintain schools that are safe and productive.

PERFORMANCE EXCEEDS CRITERIA	PERFORMANCE MEETS CRITERIA	PERFORMANCE REQUIRES IMPROVEMENT	PERFORMANCE IS UNSATISFACTORY	CANNOT JUDGE

Comments:

_____

_____

■ Domain A: Planning and Assessment

Performance Standards

A-1.   The superintendent effectively employs various processes for gathering, analyzing, and using data for decision making.

PERFORMANCE EXCEEDS CRITERIA	PERFORMANCE MEETS CRITERIA	PERFORMANCE REQUIRES IMPROVEMENT	PERFORMANCE IS UNSATISFACTORY	CANNOT JUDGE

Comments:

_____

_____

A-2.   The superintendent organizes the collaborative development and implementation of a district strategic plan based on analysis of data from a variety of sources.

PERFORMANCE EXCEEDS CRITERIA	PERFORMANCE MEETS CRITERIA	PERFORMANCE REQUIRES IMPROVEMENT	PERFORMANCE IS UNSATISFACTORY	CANNOT JUDGE

Comments:

_____

_____

A-3.   The superintendent plans, implements, supports, and assesses instructional programs that enhance teaching and student achievement of the state educational standards.

PERFORMANCE EXCEEDS CRITERIA	PERFORMANCE MEETS CRITERIA	PERFORMANCE REQUIRES IMPROVEMENT	PERFORMANCE IS UNSATISFACTORY	CANNOT JUDGE

Comments:

_____

_____

A-4.   The superintendent develops plans for effective allocation of fiscal and other resources.

PERFORMANCE EXCEEDS CRITERIA	PERFORMANCE MEETS CRITERIA	PERFORMANCE REQUIRES IMPROVEMENT	PERFORMANCE IS UNSATISFACTORY	CANNOT JUDGE

Comments:
_____
_____

■ Domain L: Instructional Leadership

Performance Standards

L-1.   The superintendent communicates a clear vision of excellence and continuous improvement consistent with the goals of the school district.

PERFORMANCE EXCEEDS CRITERIA	PERFORMANCE MEETS CRITERIA	PERFORMANCE REQUIRES IMPROVEMENT	PERFORMANCE IS UNSATISFACTORY	CANNOT JUDGE

Comments:
_____
_____

L-2.   The superintendent oversees the alignment, coordination, and delivery of assigned programs and/or curricular areas.

PERFORMANCE EXCEEDS CRITERIA	PERFORMANCE MEETS CRITERIA	PERFORMANCE REQUIRES IMPROVEMENT	PERFORMANCE IS UNSATISFACTORY	CANNOT JUDGE

Comments:
_____
_____

L-3.   The superintendent selects, inducts, supports, evaluates, and retains quality instructional and support personnel.

PERFORMANCE EXCEEDS CRITERIA	PERFORMANCE MEETS CRITERIA	PERFORMANCE REQUIRES IMPROVEMENT	PERFORMANCE IS UNSATISFACTORY	CANNOT JUDGE

Comments:
_____
_____

L-4. The superintendent provides staff development programs consistent with the program evaluation results and school instructional improvement plans.

PERFORMANCE EXCEEDS CRITERIA	PERFORMANCE MEETS CRITERIA	PERFORMANCE REQUIRES IMPROVEMENT	PERFORMANCE IS UNSATISFACTORY	CANNOT JUDGE

Comments:

_____

_____

L-5. The superintendent identifies, analyzes, and resolves problems using effective problem-solving techniques.

PERFORMANCE EXCEEDS CRITERIA	PERFORMANCE MEETS CRITERIA	PERFORMANCE REQUIRES IMPROVEMENT	PERFORMANCE IS UNSATISFACTORY	CANNOT JUDGE

Comments:

_____

_____

L-6. The superintendent assesses factors affecting student achievement and serves as an agent of change for needed improvements.

PERFORMANCE EXCEEDS CRITERIA	PERFORMANCE MEETS CRITERIA	PERFORMANCE REQUIRES IMPROVEMENT	PERFORMANCE IS UNSATISFACTORY	CANNOT JUDGE

Comments:

_____

_____

■ Domain M: Organizational Management

Performance Standards

M-1. The superintendent actively supports a safe and positive environment for students and staff.

PERFORMANCE EXCEEDS CRITERIA	PERFORMANCE MEETS CRITERIA	PERFORMANCE REQUIRES IMPROVEMENT	PERFORMANCE IS UNSATISFACTORY	CANNOT JUDGE

Comments:

_____

_____

M-2.   The superintendent develops procedures for working with the board of education that define mutual expectations, working relationships, and strategies for formulating district policies.

PERFORMANCE EXCEEDS CRITERIA	PERFORMANCE MEETS CRITERIA	PERFORMANCE REQUIRES IMPROVEMENT	PERFORMANCE IS UNSATISFACTORY	CANNOT JUDGE

Comments:

M-3.   The superintendent effectively manages human, material, and financial resources to ensure student learning and to comply with legal mandates.

PERFORMANCE EXCEEDS CRITERIA	PERFORMANCE MEETS CRITERIA	PERFORMANCE REQUIRES IMPROVEMENT	PERFORMANCE IS UNSATISFACTORY	CANNOT JUDGE

Comments:

M-4.   The superintendent demonstrates effective organizational skills to achieve school, community, and district goals.

PERFORMANCE EXCEEDS CRITERIA	PERFORMANCE MEETS CRITERIA	PERFORMANCE REQUIRES IMPROVEMENT	PERFORMANCE IS UNSATISFACTORY	CANNOT JUDGE

Comments:

M-5.   The superintendent implements sound personnel procedures in recruiting, employing, and retaining the best qualified and most competent teachers, administrators, and other personnel.

PERFORMANCE EXCEEDS CRITERIA	PERFORMANCE MEETS CRITERIA	PERFORMANCE REQUIRES IMPROVEMENT	PERFORMANCE IS UNSATISFACTORY	CANNOT JUDGE

Comments:

M-6. The superintendent provides staff development for all categories of personnel consistent with individual needs, program evaluation results, and instructional improvement plans.

PERFORMANCE EXCEEDS CRITERIA	PERFORMANCE MEETS CRITERIA	PERFORMANCE REQUIRES IMPROVEMENT	PERFORMANCE IS UNSATISFACTORY	CANNOT JUDGE

Comments:
_____
_____

M-7. The superintendent plans and implements a systematic employee performance evaluation system.

PERFORMANCE EXCEEDS CRITERIA	PERFORMANCE MEETS CRITERIA	PERFORMANCE REQUIRES IMPROVEMENT	PERFORMANCE IS UNSATISFACTORY	CANNOT JUDGE

Comments:
_____
_____

■ Domain C: Communications and Community Relations

Performance Standards

C-1. The superintendent promotes effective communication and interpersonal relations within the school district.

PERFORMANCE EXCEEDS CRITERIA	PERFORMANCE MEETS CRITERIA	PERFORMANCE REQUIRES IMPROVEMENT	PERFORMANCE IS UNSATISFACTORY	CANNOT JUDGE

Comments:
_____
_____

C-2. The superintendent establishes and maintains effective channels of communication with board members and between the schools and community, strengthening support of constituencies and building coalitions.

PERFORMANCE EXCEEDS CRITERIA	PERFORMANCE MEETS CRITERIA	PERFORMANCE REQUIRES IMPROVEMENT	PERFORMANCE IS UNSATISFACTORY	CANNOT JUDGE

Comments:
_____
_____

C-3. The superintendent works collaboratively with staff, families, and community members to secure resources and to support the success of a diverse student population.

PERFORMANCE EXCEEDS CRITERIA	PERFORMANCE MEETS CRITERIA	PERFORMANCE REQUIRES IMPROVEMENT	PERFORMANCE IS UNSATISFACTORY	CANNOT JUDGE

Comments:

_____

_____

C-4. The superintendent creates an atmosphere of trust and mutual respect with staff and community.

PERFORMANCE EXCEEDS CRITERIA	PERFORMANCE MEETS CRITERIA	PERFORMANCE REQUIRES IMPROVEMENT	PERFORMANCE IS UNSATISFACTORY	CANNOT JUDGE

Comments:

_____

_____

■ Domain P: Professionalism

Performance Standards

P-1. The superintendent models professional, moral, and ethical standards as well as personal integrity in all interactions.

PERFORMANCE EXCEEDS CRITERIA	PERFORMANCE MEETS CRITERIA	PERFORMANCE REQUIRES IMPROVEMENT	PERFORMANCE IS UNSATISFACTORY	CANNOT JUDGE

Comments:

_____

_____

P-2. The superintendent works in a collegial and collaborative manner with school personnel and the community to promote and support the mission and goals of the school district.

PERFORMANCE EXCEEDS CRITERIA	PERFORMANCE MEETS CRITERIA	PERFORMANCE REQUIRES IMPROVEMENT	PERFORMANCE IS UNSATISFACTORY	CANNOT JUDGE

Comments:

_____

_____

P-3. The superintendent takes responsibility for and participates in a meaningful and continuous process of professional development that results in the enhancement of student learning.

PERFORMANCE EXCEEDS CRITERIA	PERFORMANCE MEETS CRITERIA	PERFORMANCE REQUIRES IMPROVEMENT	PERFORMANCE IS UNSATISFACTORY	CANNOT JUDGE

Comments:

_____

_____

P-4. The superintendent provides service to the profession, the district, and the community.

PERFORMANCE EXCEEDS CRITERIA	PERFORMANCE MEETS CRITERIA	PERFORMANCE REQUIRES IMPROVEMENT	PERFORMANCE IS UNSATISFACTORY	CANNOT JUDGE

Comments:

_____

_____

■ Evaluation Summary ■

■ Strengths

■ Areas for Improvement

Signatures:

_____   _____
Superintendent   School Board Chair

_____   _____
Date   Date

SUPERINTENDENT'S SIGNATURE ACKNOWLEDGES RECEIPT OF THIS FORM.
WRITTEN COMMENTS MAY BE ATTACHED.
COMMENTS ATTACHED: ____ YES ____ NO

Appendix H

Sample
Summative Evaluation Form II

Appendix H

■ 4-level rating scale (7 pages) ■

Superintendent Summative Evaluation

Superintendent's Name _____

Evaluator _____

Academic/Fiscal Year _____

<u>DIRECTIONS</u>

To be completed by the School Board as documentation of the superintendent's annual evaluation.

■ Domain G: Policy and Governance

Performance Standards	Performance Exceeds Criteria	Performance Meets Criteria	Performance Requires Improvement	Performance Is Unsatisfactory	Cannot Judge
G-1 The superintendent works with the school board to develop and implement policies that define organizational expectations.					
G-2 The superintendent functions as the primary instructional leader for the school district, relying on support from staff as necessary when advising the school board.					
G-3 The superintendent oversees the administration of the school district's day-to-day operations.					
G-4 The superintendent works with all individuals, groups, agencies, committees, and organizations to provide and maintain schools that are safe and productive.					

Comments _____

_____

_____

_____

_____

_____

_____

_____

_____

_____

_____

■ **Domain L: Instructional Leadership**

Performance Standards	Performance Exceeds Criteria	Performance Meets Criteria	Performance Requires Improvement	Performance Is Unsatisfactory	Cannot Judge
L-1 The superintendent communicates a clear vision of excellence and continuous improvement consistent with the goals of the school district.					
L-2 The superintendent oversees the alignment, coordination, and delivery of assigned programs and/or curricular areas.					
L-3 The superintendent selects, inducts, supports, evaluates, and retains quality instructional and support personnel.					
L-4 The superintendent provides staff development programs consistent with the program evaluation results and school instructional improvement plans.					
L-5 The superintendent identifies, analyzes, and resolves problems using effective problem-solving techniques.					
L-6 The superintendent assesses factors affecting student achievement and serves as an agent of change for needed improvements.					

Comments

_____

_____

_____

_____

_____

_____

_____

_____

_____

_____

■ **Domain M: Organizational Management**

Performance Standards	Performance Exceeds Criteria	Performance Meets Criteria	Performance Requires Improvement	Performance Is Unsatisfactory	Cannot Judge
M-1 The superintendent actively supports a safe and positive environment for students and staff.					
M-2 The superintendent develops procedures for working with the board of education that define mutual expectations, working relationships, and strategies for formulating district policies.					
M-3 The superintendent effectively manages human, material, and financial resources to ensure student learning and to comply with legal mandates.					
M-4 The superintendent demonstrates effective organizational skills to achieve school, community, and district goals.					
M-5 The superintendent implements sound personnel procedures in recruiting, employing, and retaining the best qualified and most competent teachers, administrators, and other personnel.					
M-6 The superintendent provides staff development for all categories of personnel consistent with individual needs, program evaluation results, and instructional improvement plans.					
M-7 The superintendent plans and implements a systematic employee performance evaluation system.					

Comments

_____

_____

_____

_____

■ Domain C: Communications and Community Relations

Performance Standards	Performance Exceeds Criteria	Performance Meets Criteria	Performance Requires Improvement	Performance Is Unsatisfactory	Cannot Judge
C-1 The superintendent promotes effective communication and interpersonal relations within the school district.					
C-2 The superintendent establishes and maintains effective channels of communication with board members and between the schools and community, strengthening support of constituencies and building coalitions.					
C-3 The superintendent works collaboratively with staff, families, and community members to secure resources and to support the success of a diverse student population.					
C-4 The superintendent creates an atmosphere of trust and mutual respect with staff and community.					

Comments

■ Domain A: Planning and Assessment

Performance Standards	Performance Exceeds Criteria	Performance Meets Criteria	Performance Requires Improvement	Performance Is Unsatisfactory	Cannot Judge
A-1 The superintendent effectively employs various processes for gathering, analyzing, and using data for decision making.					
A-2 The superintendent organizes the collaborative development and implementation of a district strategic plan based on analysis of data from a variety of sources.					
A-3 The superintendent plans, implements, supports, and assesses instructional programs that enhance teaching and student achievement of the state educational standards.					
A-4 The superintendent develops plans for effective allocation of fiscal and other resources.					

Comments

■ **Domain P: Professionalism**

Performance Standards	Performance Exceeds Criteria	Performance Meets Criteria	Performance Requires Improvement	Performance Is Unsatisfactory	Cannot Judge
P-1 The superintendent models professional, moral, and ethical standards as well as personal integrity in all interactions.					
P-2 The superintendent works in a collegial and collaborative manner with school personnel and the community to promote and support the mission and goals of the school district.					
P-3 The superintendent takes responsibility for and participates in a meaningful and continuous process of professional development that results in the enhancement of student learning.					
P-4 The superintendent provides service to the profession, the district, and the community.					

Comments
_____
_____
_____
_____
_____
_____
_____
_____
_____
_____
_____
_____
_____
_____
_____
_____

■ Evaluation Summary ■

■ Strengths

■ Areas for Improvement

Signatures:

_____   _____
Superintendent   School Board Chair

_____   _____
Date   Date

SUPERINTENDENT'S SIGNATURE ACKNOWLEDGES RECEIPT OF THIS FORM.
WRITTEN COMMENTS MAY BE ATTACHED.
COMMENTS ATTACHED: ____ YES   ____ NO

■ Evaluation Summary ■

■ Strengths

■ Areas for Improvement

Signatures:

_____   _____
Superintendent   School Board Chair

_____   _____
Date   Date

SUPERINTENDENT'S SIGNATURE ACKNOWLEDGES RECEIPT OF THIS FORM.
WRITTEN COMMENTS MAY BE ATTACHED.
COMMENTS ATTACHED: ____ YES ____ NO

■ 3-level rating scale (4 pages) ■

Superintendent Summative Evaluation

Superintendent's Name _____

Evaluator _____

Academic/Fiscal Year _____

DIRECTIONS

To be completed by the School Board as documentation of the superintendent's evaluation.

Domain G: Policy and Governance Performance Standards	Performance Exceeds Criteria	Performance Meets Criteria	Has Not Met Performance Criteria	Cannot Judge
G-1. The superintendent works with the school board to develop and implement policies that define organizational expectations.				
G-2. The superintendent functions as the primary instructional leader for the school district, relying on support from staff as necessary when advising the school board.				
G-3. The superintendent oversees the administration of the school district's day-to-day operations.				
G-4. The superintendent works with all individuals, groups, agencies, committees, and organizations to provide and maintain schools that are safe and productive.				
Domain A: Planning and Assessment Performance Standards				
A-1. The superintendent effectively employs various processes for gathering, analyzing, and using data for decision making.				
A-2. The superintendent organizes the collaborative development and implementation of a district strategic plan based on analysis of data from a variety of sources.				
A-3. The superintendent plans, implements, supports, and assesses instructional programs that enhance teaching and student achievement of the state educational standards.				
A-4. The superintendent develops plans for effective allocation of fiscal and other resources.				

Domain L: Instructional Leadership **Performance Standards**	Performance Exceeds Criteria	Performance Meets Criteria	Has Not Met Performance Criteria	Cannot Judge
L-1. The superintendent communicates a clear vision of excellence and continuous improvement consistent with the goals of the school district.				
L-2. The superintendent oversees the alignment, coordination, and delivery of assigned programs and/or curricular areas.				
L-3. The superintendent selects, inducts, supports, evaluates, and retains quality instructional and support personnel.				
L-4. The superintendent provides staff development programs consistent with the program evaluation results and school instructional improvement plans.				
L-5. The superintendent identifies, analyzes, and resolves problems using effective problem-solving techniques.				
L-6. The superintendent assesses factors affecting student achievement and serves as an agent of change for needed improvements.				
Domain M: Organizational Management **Performance Standards**				
M-1. The superintendent actively supports a safe and positive environment for students and staff.				
M-2. The superintendent develops procedures for working with the board of education that define mutual expectations, working relationships, and strategies for formulating district policies.				
M-3. The superintendent effectively manages human, material, and financial resources to ensure student learning and to comply with legal mandates.				
M-4. The superintendent demonstrates effective organizational skills to achieve school, community, and district goals.				
M-5. The superintendent implements sound personnel procedures in recruiting, employing, and retaining the best qualified and most competent teachers, administrators, and other personnel.				
M-6. The superintendent provides staff development for all categories of personnel consistent with individual needs, program evaluation results, and instructional improvement plans.				
M-7. The superintendent plans and implements a systematic employee performance evaluation system.				

Domain C: Communications & Community Relations Performance Standards	Performance Exceeds Criteria	Performance Meets Criteria	Has Not Met Performance Criteria	Cannot Judge
C-1. The superintendent promotes effective communication and interpersonal relations within the school district.				
C-2. The superintendent establishes and maintains effective channels of communication with board members and between the schools and community, strengthening support of constituencies and building coalitions.				
C-3. The superintendent works collaboratively with staff, families, and community members to secure resources and to support the success of a diverse student population.				
C-4. The superintendent creates an atmosphere of trust and mutual respect with staff and community.				
Domain P: Professionalism **Performance Standards**				
P-1. The superintendent models professional, moral, and ethical standards as well as personal integrity in all interactions.				
P-2. The superintendent works in a collegial and collaborative manner with school personnel and the community to promote and support the mission and goals of the school district.				
P-3. The superintendent takes responsibility for and participates in a meaningful and continuous process of professional development that results in the enhancement of student learning.				
P-4. The superintendent provides service to the profession, the district, and the community.				

Comments _____

_____

_____

_____

_____

_____

_____

Appendix I

Sample
Summative Evaluation Form III

Superintendent Summative Evaluation

_____   _____
Superintendent   Academic Year

Directions: The evaluation is to be completed by the School Board as documentation of the
superintendent's annual evaluation. Based upon evidence gathered through
appropriate sources, select the rating for each job responsibility that most closely
describes the superintendent's performance. Add comments where appropriate.

Domain G: POLICY & GOVERNANCE	Exceeds Expectations	Meets Expectations	Needs Assistance	Unsatisfactory
Performance Standards				
G-1 The superintendent works with the school board to develop and implement policies that define organizational expectations.	☐	☐	☐	☐
G-2 The superintendent functions as the primary instructional leader for the school district, relying on support from staff as necessary when advising the school board.	☐	☐	☐	☐
G-3 The superintendent oversees the administration of the school district's day-to-day operations.	☐	☐	☐	☐
G-4 The superintendent works with all individuals, groups, agencies, committees, and organizations to provide and maintain schools that are safe and productive.	☐	☐	☐	☐

Comments: _____
_____
_____
_____
_____

Domain A: PLANNING & ASSESSMENT	Exceeds Expectations	Meets Expectations	Needs Assistance	Unsatisfactory
Performance Standards				
A-1 The superintendent effectively employs various processes for gathering, analyzing, and using data for decision making.	☐	☐	☐	☐
A-2 The superintendent organizes the collaborative development and implementation of a district strategic plan based on analysis of data from a variety of sources.	☐	☐	☐	☐
A-3 The superintendent plans, implements, supports, and assesses instructional programs that enhance teaching and student achievement of the state educational standards.	☐	☐	☐	☐
A-4 The superintendent develops plans for effective allocation of fiscal and other resources.	☐	☐	☐	☐

Comments: _____

_____

_____

_____

_____

_____

_____

_____

_____

_____

_____

_____

_____

_____

Domain L: INSTRUCTIONAL LEADERSHIP	Exceeds Expectations	Meets Expectations	Needs Assistance	Unsatisfactory
Performance Standards				
L-1 The superintendent communicates a clear vision of excellence and continuous improvement consistent with the goals of the school district.	☐	☐	☐	☐
L-2 The superintendent oversees the alignment, coordination, and delivery of assigned programs and/or curricular areas.	☐	☐	☐	☐
L-3 The superintendent selects, inducts, supports, evaluates, and retains quality instructional and support personnel.	☐	☐	☐	☐
L-4 The superintendent provides staff development programs consistent with program evaluation results and school instructional improvement plans.	☐	☐	☐	☐
L-5 The superintendent identifies, analyzes, and resolves problems using effective problem-solving techniques.	☐	☐	☐	☐
L-6 The superintendent assesses factors affecting student achievement and serves as an agent of change for needed improvements.	☐	☐	☐	☐

Comments: _____

_____

_____

_____

_____

_____

_____

Domain M:
ORGANIZATIONAL
MANAGEMENT

Performance Standards

	Exceeds Expectations	Meets Expectations	Needs Assistance	Unsatisfactory
M-1 The superintendent actively supports a safe and positive environment for students and staff.	☐	☐	☐	☐
M-2 The superintendent develops procedures for working with the board of education that define mutual expectations, working relationships, and strategies for formulating district policies.	☐	☐	☐	☐
M-3 The superintendent effectively manages human, material, and financial resources to ensure student learning and to comply with legal mandates.	☐	☐	☐	☐
M-4 The superintendent demonstrates effective organizational skills to achieve school, community, and district goals.	☐	☐	☐	☐
M-5 The superintendent implements sound personnel procedures in recruiting, employing, and retaining the best qualified and most competent teachers, administrators, and other personnel.	☐	☐	☐	☐
M-6 The superintendent provides staff development for all categories of personnel consistent with individual needs, program evaluation results, and instructional improvement plans.	☐	☐	☐	☐
M-7 The superintendent plans and implements a systematic employee performance evaluation system.	☐	☐	☐	☐

Comments: _____

_____

Domain C: **COMMUNICATIONS** **& COMMUNITY** **RELATIONS**	Exceeds Expectations	Meets Expectations	Needs Assistance	Unsatisfactory
Performance Standards				
C-1 The superintendent promotes effective communication and interpersonal relations within the school district.	☐	☐	☐	☐
C-2 The superintendent establishes and maintains effective channels of communication with board members and between the schools and community, strengthening support of constituencies and building coalitions.	☐	☐	☐	☐
C-3 The superintendent works collaboratively with staff, families, and community members to secure resources and to support the success of a diverse student population.	☐	☐	☐	☐
C-4 The superintendent creates an atmosphere of trust and mutual respect with staff and community.	☐	☐	☐	☐

Comments: _____

_____

_____

_____

_____

_____

_____

_____

_____

_____

Domain P: PROFESSIONALISM	Exceeds Expectations	Meets Expectations	Needs Assistance	Unsatisfactory
Performance Standards				
P-1 The superintendent models professional, moral, and ethical standards as well as personal integrity in all interactions.	☐	☐	☐	☐
P-2 The superintendent works in a collegial and collaborative manner with school personnel and the community to promote and support the mission and goals of the school district.	☐	☐	☐	☐
P-3 The superintendent takes responsibility for and participates in a meaningful and continuous process of professional development that results in the enhancement of student learning.	☐	☐	☐	☐
P-4 The superintendent provides service to the profession, the district, and the community.	☐	☐	☐	☐

Comments: _____

_____

_____

_____

_____

_____

_____

_____

_____

_____

_____

_____

_____

Strengths

Areas for Continuous Improvement

Board Member Signatures

_____   _____

_____   _____

_____   Date: _____

Superintendent Signature*

_____   Date: _____

_____

* Written comments may be attached. If comments are attached, initial and date here. _____

■ 3-level rating scale (4 pages) ■

Superintendent Summative Evaluation

_____   _____
         Superintendent   Academic Year

Directions: The evaluation is to be completed by the School Board as documentation of the superintendent's annual evaluation. Based upon evidence gathered through appropriate sources, select the rating for each job responsibility that most closely describes the superintendent's performance. Add comments where appropriate.

Domain G: POLICY & GOVERNANCE	**Exceeds Expectations**	**Meets Expectations**	**Has Not Met Expectations**
Performance Standards			
G-1 The superintendent works with the school board to develop and implement policies that define organizational expectations.	☐	☐	☐
G-2 The superintendent functions as the primary instructional leader for the school district, relying on support from staff as necessary when advising the school board.	☐	☐	☐
G-3 The superintendent oversees the administration of the school district's day-to-day operations.	☐	☐	☐
G-4 The superintendent works with all individuals, groups, agencies, committees, and organizations to provide and maintain schools that are safe and productive.	☐	☐	☐

Domain A: PLANNING & ASSESSMENT

Performance Standards

	Exceeds Expectations	**Meets Expectations**	**Has Not Met Expectations**
A-1 The superintendent effectively employs various processes for gathering, analyzing, and using data for decision making.	☐	☐	☐
A-2 The superintendent organizes the collaborative development and implementation of a district strategic plan based on analysis of data from a variety of sources.	☐	☐	☐
A-3 The superintendent plans, implements, supports, and assesses instructional programs that enhance teaching and student achievement of the state educational standards.	☐	☐	☐
A-4 The superintendent develops plans for effective allocation of fiscal and other resources.	☐	☐	☐

Domain L: INSTRUCTIONAL LEADERSHIP	Exceeds Expectations	Meets Expectations	Has Not Met Expectations
Performance Standards			
L-1 The superintendent communicates a clear vision of excellence and continuous improvement consistent with the goals of the school district.	❑	❑	❑
L-2 The superintendent oversees the alignment, coordination, and delivery of assigned programs and/or curricular areas.	❑	❑	❑
L-3 The superintendent selects, inducts, supports, evaluates, and retains quality instructional and support personnel.	❑	❑	❑
L-4 The superintendent provides staff development programs consistent with program evaluation results and school instructional improvement plans.	❑	❑	❑
L-5 The superintendent identifies, analyzes, and resolves problems using effective problem-solving techniques.	❑	❑	❑
L-6 The superintendent assesses factors affecting student achievement and serves as an agent of change for needed improvements.	❑	❑	❑

Domain M: ORGANIZATIONAL MANAGEMENT

Performance Standards

M-1 The superintendent actively supports a safe and positive environment for students and staff.	☐	☐	☐
M-2 The superintendent develops procedures for working with the board of education that define mutual expectations, working relationships, and strategies for formulating district policies.	☐	☐	☐
M-3 The superintendent effectively manages human, material, and financial resources to ensure student learning and to comply with legal mandates.	☐	☐	☐
M-4 The superintendent demonstrates effective organizational skills to achieve school, community, and district goals.	☐	☐	☐
M-5. The superintendent implements sound personnel procedures in recruiting, employing, and retaining the best qualified and most competent teachers, administrators, and other personnel.	☐	☐	☐
M-6. The superintendent provides staff development for all categories of personnel consistent with individual needs, program evaluation results, and instructional improvement plans.	☐	☐	☐
M-7. The superintendent plans and implements a systematic employee performance evaluation system.	☐	☐	☐

Domain C: COMMUNICATIONS & COMMUNITY RELATIONS

Performance Standards	Exceeds Expectations	Meets Expectations	Has Not Met Expectations
C-1 The superintendent promotes effective communication and interpersonal relations within the school district.	☐	☐	☐
C-2 The superintendent establishes and maintains effective channels of communication with board members and between the schools and community, strengthening support of constituencies and building coalitions.	☐	☐	☐
C-3 The superintendent works collaboratively with staff, families, and community members to secure resources and to support the success of a diverse student population.	☐	☐	☐
C-4 The superintendent creates an atmosphere of trust and mutual respect with staff and community.	☐	☐	☐

Domain P: PROFESSIONALISM

Performance Standards	Exceeds Expectations	Meets Expectations	Has Not Met Expectations
P-1 The superintendent models professional, moral, and ethical standards as well as personal integrity in all interactions.	☐	☐	☐
P-2 The superintendent works in a collegial and collaborative manner with school personnel and the community to promote and support the mission and goals of the school district.	☐	☐	☐
P-3 The superintendent takes responsibility for and participates in a meaningful and continuous process of professional development that results in the enhancement of student learning.	☐	☐	☐
P-4 The superintendent provides service to the profession, the district, and the community.	☐	☐	☐

Notes

_____

_____

_____

_____

_____

_____

_____

_____

_____

_____

Strengths

Areas for Continuous Improvement

Board Member Signatures

_____   _____

_____   _____

_____   Date: _____

Superintendent Signature＊

_____   Date: _____

＊Written comments may be attached. If comments are attached, initial and date here. _____

Appendix J

Sample
Summative Evaluation Form IV

Appendix J

■ 4-level rating scale (3 pages) ■

Superintendent Summative Evaluation

_____   _____
Superintendent   Academic Year

Directions: The evaluation is to be completed by the School Board as documentation of the superintendent's annual evaluation. Based upon evidence gathered through appropriate sources, select the rating for each job responsibility that most closely describes the superintendent's performance. Add comments where appropriate.

Domain G: **POLICY AND GOVERNANCE**	Exceeds Expectations	Meets Expectations	Needs Assistance	Unsatisfactory
	☐	☐	☐	☐

Comments: _____

_____

_____

_____

_____

_____

Domain A: **PLANNING AND ASSESSMENT**	Exceeds Expectations	Meets Expectations	Needs Assistance	Unsatisfactory
	☐	☐	☐	☐

Comments: _____

_____

_____

_____

_____

_____

_____

_____

Domain L: INSTRUCTIONAL LEADERSHIP	Exceeds Expectations	Meets Expectations	Needs Assistance	Unsatisfactory
	☐	☐	☐	☐

Comments: _____

_____

_____

_____

_____

_____

_____

Domain M: ORGANIZATIONAL MANAGEMENT	Exceeds Expectations	Meets Expectations	Needs Assistance	Unsatisfactory
	☐	☐	☐	☐

Comments: _____

_____

_____

_____

_____

_____

_____

Domain C: COMMUNICATIONS AND COMMUNITY RELATIONS	Exceeds Expectations	Meets Expectations	Needs Assistance	Unsatisfactory
	☐	☐	☐	☐

Comments: _____

_____

_____

_____

_____

_____

_____

Domain P: PROFESSIONALISM	Exceeds Expectations	Meets Expectations	Needs Assistance	Unsatisfactory
	☐	☐	☐	☐

Comments: _____

_____

_____

_____

_____

_____

_____

Strengths

Areas for Continuous Improvement

Board Member Signatures

_____   _____

_____   _____

_____   Date: _____

Superintendent Signature[1]

_____   Date: _____

---

[1] Written comments may be attached. If comments are attached, initial and date here. _____

■ 3-level rating scale (3 pages) ■

Superintendent Summative Evaluation

_____   _____
          Superintendent   Academic Year

Directions: The evaluation is to be completed by the School Board as documentation of the superintendent's annual evaluation. Based upon evidence gathered through appropriate sources, select the rating for each job responsibility that most closely describes the superintendent's performance. Add comments where appropriate.

Domain G: POLICY AND GOVERNANCE	Exceeds Expectations	Meets Expectations	Has Not Met Expectations
	☐	☐	☐

Comments: _____

_____

_____

_____

_____

_____

_____

_____

Domain A: PLANNING AND ASSESSMENT	Exceeds Expectations	Meets Expectations	Has Not Met Expectations
	☐	☐	☐

Comments: _____

_____

_____

_____

_____

_____

_____

_____

_____

_____

Domain L: **INSTRUCTIONAL** **LEADERSHIP**	Exceeds Expectations ☐	Meets Expectations ☐	Has Not Met Expectations ☐

Comments: _____

_____

_____

_____

_____

_____

_____

Domain M: **ORGANIZATIONAL** **MANAGEMENT**	Exceeds Expectations ☐	Meets Expectations ☐	Has Not Met Expectations ☐

Comments: _____

_____

_____

_____

_____

_____

_____

Domain C: **COMMUNICATIONS** **AND COMMUNITY** **RELATIONS**	Exceeds Expectations ☐	Meets Expectations ☐	Has Not Met Expectations ☐

Comments: _____

_____

_____

_____

_____

_____

_____

_____

_____

Domain P: **PROFESSIONALISM**	**Exceeds** Expectations	**Meets** Expectations	**Has Not Met** Expectations
	☐	☐	☐

Comments: _____

_____

_____

_____

_____

_____

_____

Strengths

Areas for Continuous Improvement

Board Member Signatures

_____   _____

_____   _____

_____   Date: _____

Superintendent Signature*

_____   Date: _____

_____

* Written comments may be attached. If comments are attached, initial and date here. _____

Appendix K

Sample
Board of Education Policy:
Evaluation of the Superintendent

The Board of Education, in compliance with state law, will evaluate the Superintendent at least annually. Each evaluation shall be in writing, a copy shall be provided to the Superintendent, and the Superintendent and the board shall meet to discuss the findings. The evaluations shall be based upon the goals and objectives of the district, the responsibilities of the Superintendent and such other criteria as the State Board of Education shall by regulation prescribe.

The purpose of the evaluation shall be:

A. To promote professional excellence and improve the skills of the Superintendent.
B. To improve the quality of the education received by the students served by the public schools of the district.
C. To provide a basis for the review of the job performance of the Superintendent.

ROLE AND RESPONSIBILITY OF THE BOARD

The role and responsibility of the board in the evaluation of the Superintendent shall be:

1. To ensure that each member completes the School Boards Association training program on the evaluation of the Superintendent within six months of the commencement of newly appointed or elected district board member's term of office.

2. After consultation with the Superintendent, to determine the roles and responsibilities for the implementation of this policy and attendant procedures.
3. After consultation with the Superintendent, to prepare an individual plan for professional growth and development of the Superintendent based in part upon any needs identified in the evaluation. This plan shall be mutually developed by the board and the Superintendent.
4. To ensure that all non-conflicted members of the board shall prepare an annual performance report and convene an annual summary conference between the Superintendent and a majority of the full membership of the board.
5. To hold an annual summary conference with a majority of the total membership of the board and the Superintendent. The annual summary conference shall be held before the written performance report is filed. The conference shall be held in executive session, unless the Superintendent, subsequent to adequate notice, requests that it be held in public. The conference shall include, but not be limited to, review of the following:
   a. Performance of the Superintendent based upon the job description.
   b. Progress of the Superintendent in achieving and/or implementing the school district's goals, program objectives, policies, instructional priorities, State goals, and statutory requirements.
   c. Indicators of student progress and growth toward program objectives.
6. To prepare, by July 1, subsequent to the annual summary conference, an annual written performance report. The annual written summary performance report shall be prepared by the Board President or designee of the board and provided to the Superintendent. This report shall include, but not be limited to:
   a. Performance areas of strength.
   b. Performance areas needing improvement based upon the job description and evaluation criteria in "E" above.
   c. Recommendations for professional growth and development.
   d. A summary of available indicators of pupil progress and growth and a statement of how these available indicators relate to the effectiveness of the overall program and the performance of the Superintendent.
   e. An option for the Superintendent, within 10 days of receipt of the report, to include for performance data which has not been included in the report prepared by the Board President or designee to be entered into the record by the Superintendent.

The board shall add to the Superintendent's personnel file, all written performance reports and supporting data, including, but not limited to, indicators of student progress and growth to a Superintendent's personnel file. The records shall be confidential and not be subject to public inspection or copying pursuant to the Open Public Records Act.

The board may determine whether the services of a qualified consultant will contribute substantially to the evaluation process and to engage such a consultant as deemed appropriate to assist the board. The evaluation itself shall be the responsibility of the board.

ROLE AND RESPONSIBILITY OF THE SUPERINTENDENT

The board shall determine the roles and responsibilities of the Superintendent in consultation with the Superintendent. The Superintendent shall provide information and propose procedures for:

1. The development of a job description and evaluation criteria, based upon the district's local goals, program objectives, policies, instructional priorities, state goals, statutory requirements, and the functions, duties and responsibilities of the Superintendent. The evaluation criteria shall include but not be limited to available indicators of pupil progress.
2. Specification of methods of data collection and reporting appropriate to the job description.
3. Design of evaluation instruments suited to reviewing the Superintendent's performance based upon the job description.
4. Establishing an evaluation calendar to include a date for the annual conference and including appropriate information to allow proper consideration of all the items to be included in the subsequent written performance report.
5. After the board's preparation of the annual written performance report, to provide all other appropriate information relative to evaluation of his/her performance not contained in the report.
6. Preparation and review of the Professional Growth Plan for the administrator's professional development.

The policy shall be delivered to the Superintendent upon adoption. Amendments to the policy shall be distributed within 10 working days after adoption.

Adopted:

Key Words

Superintendent Evaluation, Superintendent Job Description, CSA, Superintendent, Evaluation

Legal References:

Appendix L

Sample
Board of Education Procedures

Evaluation of the Superintendent

Members of the Board of Education and superintendent will implement the following procedures:

1. The Board of Education and the superintendent shall jointly identify, in May of each school year, goals and priorities of the district for the coming year.
2. The Board of Education and the superintendent shall jointly identify, in June of each school year, the superintendent's personal goals, including student achievement goals, for the coming year.
3. The superintendent will develop an action plan for goal achievement. Each action plan will describe the major activities involved in achieving the objective, a timeline, and indicators of success.
4. By the end of July, the Board will review each plan and, after discussion, each plan will be approved, modified, or dropped. Upon approval, the superintendent will be required to implement the plans.
5. By the end of August, the Board and the superintendent will review the performance standards and evaluative instruments, the format for reviewing progress toward district goals, and the calendar of events that will lead to the completion of the evaluation.
6. By October 15, the superintendent is expected to provide the Board with a report on the progress being made on each goal at a scheduled closed-session meeting.
7. By January 1, the superintendent is expected to provide the board with a report on the progress being made on each goal at a scheduled closed-session meeting. At this time the Board will provide feedback to the superintendent in an interim review of progress.

8. By March 15, the superintendent is expected to provide the Board with a report on the progress being made on each goal at a scheduled closed-session meeting.
9. By April 30, the superintendent's performance, including goal achievement, will be assessed via a summative evaluation by the Board. A discussion between the superintendent and Board will provide an opportunity for the superintendent to provide an explanation for lack of goal achievement and for the Board to provide commendations if appropriate and suggestions for improvement.
10. Board members shall annually conduct a self-evaluation to determine the degree to which they are meeting their responsibilities as board members and the educational needs of the school community.

Adapted from New Jersey School Boards Association, http://www.njsba.org !Field_Services/SR/policy.html.

Summary Tables

Superintendent Evaluation State by State

Summary Rubric Results for All Standards by State

State	Propriety	Utility	Accuracy	Feasibility	Total Score
Alabama	-	-	-	-	-
Alaska	-	-	-	-	-
Arizona	0.5	0	1	0	1.5
Arkansas	-	-	-	-	-
California	-	-	-	-	-
Colorado	-	-	-	-	-
Connecticut	1.5	0	1	1	3.5
Delaware	2.5	6	5.5	2	16
Florida	-	-	-	-	-
Georgia	2	2	1.5	1	6.5
Hawaii	2	6	3	1	12
Idaho	0	3	1	1	5
Illinois	1.5	1	1	0	3.5
Indiana	-	-	-	-	-
Iowa	1	6	3	1	11
Kansas	3	6	4	1	14
Kentucky	1	0	1.5	0	2.5
Louisiana	-	-	-	-	-
Maine	-	-	-	-	-
Maryland	-	-	-	-	-
Massachusetts	4.5	6	6	2	18.5
Michigan	4.5	4	6.5	2	17
Minnesota	-	-	-	-	-
Mississippi	2	4.5	3	1	10.5
Missouri	1.5	3	3.5	0.5	8.5
Montana	1.5	3.5	2.5	1	8.5
Nebraska	1	2.5	1	1	5.5
Nevada	-	-	-	-	-
New Hampshire	0	0	1	1	2
New Jersey	4.5	6	3	1	14.5
New Mexico	-	-	-	-	-
New York	1	0	1	2	4
North Carolina	2	4	4.5	1	11.5
North Dakota	0	1	1	1	3
Ohio	1	3.5	2.5	0.5	7.5
Oklahoma	0	2.5	2	1	5.5

Oregon	-	-	-	-	-
Pennsylvania	0.5	2.5	1	0	4.0
Rhode Island	1	0	1	0	2
South Carolina	0	1	1	0	2
South Dakota	-	-	-	-	-
Tennessee	0	2	1	1	4
Texas	1	2	2.5	1	6.5
Utah	-	-	-	-	-
Vermont	-	-	-	-	-
Virginia	2.5	5	3	1	11.5
Washington	2	1	2	2	7
West Virginia	4.5	4	3	1	12.5
Wisconsin	0	0	2	0	2
Wyoming	1.5	5	3.5	1	11
Washington D.C.	0	0	1	1	2
Total Possible Point Value	6	7	10	2	25

Summary Rubric Results for the Propriety Standard by State

State	Indicator A	Indicator B	Indicator C	Indicator D	Indicator E	Indicator F	Total Score
Alabama	-	-	-	-	-	-	-
Alaska	-	-	-	-	-	-	-
Arizona	0	0	0	0	.5	0	0.5
Arkansas	-	-	-	-	-	-	-
California	-	-	-	-	-	-	-
Colorado	-	-	-	-	-	-	-
Connecticut	0	0	0	0	.5	1	1.5
Delaware	0	1	1	0	.5	0	2.5
Florida	-	-	-	-	-	-	-
Georgia	0	1	0	0	0	1	2
Hawaii	0	0	0	0	1	1	2
Idaho	0	0	0	0	0	0	0
Illinois	0	0	0	0	.5	1	1.5
Indiana	-	-	-	-	-	-	-
Iowa	0	0	0	.5	.5	0	1
Kansas	0	0	1	.5	.5	1	3
Kentucky	0	0	0	0	0	1	1
Louisiana	-	-	-	-	-	-	-
Maine	-	-	-	-	-	-	-
Maryland	-	-	-	-	-	-	-
Massachusetts	0	1	1	.5	1	1	4.5
Michigan	0	1	1	.5	1	1	4.5
Minnesota	-	-	-	-	-	-	-
Mississippi	0	0	0	1	1	0	2
Missouri	0	0	0	.5	0	1	1.5
Montana	0	0	0	0	.5	1	1.5
Nebraska	0	0	1	0	0	0	1
Nevada	-	-	-	-	-	-	0
New Hampshire	0	0	0	0	0	0	0
New Jersey	0	1	.5	1	1	1	4.5
New Mexico	-	-	-	-	-	-	-
New York	0	0	1	0	0	0	1
North Carolina	0	1	0	0	1	0	2
North Dakota	0	0	0	0	0	0	0
Ohio	0	0	0	.5	.5	0	1
Oklahoma	0	0	0	0	0	0	0
Oregon	-	-	-	-	-	-	-
Pennsylvania	0	0	0	0	0	.5	0.5
Rhode Island	0	1	0	0	0	0	1
South Carolina	0	0	0	0	0	0	0
South Dakota	-	-	-	-	-	-	0
Tennessee	0	0	0	0	0	0	0
Texas	0	0	0	0	1	0	1
Utah	-	-	-	-	-	-	-
Vermont	-	-	-	-	-	-	-
Virginia	0	1	0	.5	1	0	2.5
Washington	0	0	1	0	0	1	2
West Virginia	0	1	1	1	.5	1	4.5
Wisconsin	0	0	0	0	0	0	0
Wyoming	0	.5	1	0	0	0	1.5
Washington D.C.	0	0	0	0	0	0	0

Data Collection Procedures: Evaluators
Indicator A: Does the state mandate exclusion of evaluators who may have a conflict of interest within the superintendent process?
Indicator B: Does the state mandate training for evaluators in conducting a superintendent evaluation?
Indicator C: Does the state mandate any additional oversight to ensure evaluators implement the superintendent evaluation system with fidelity?
Data Collection Procedures: Stakeholder Involvement & Communication
Indicator D: Does the state require or permit involvement of professional educational associations in development of the superintendent evaluation policy?
Indicator E: Does the state require or permit non-board member stakeholder participation in the superintendent evaluation?
Methods for Using Results
Indicator F: Does the state mandate confidentiality or public disclosure of the superintendent evaluation?

Summary Rubric Results for the Utility Standard by State

State	Indicator A	Indicator B	Indicator C	Indicator D	Indicator E	Indicator F	Indicator G	Total Score
Alabama	-	-	-	-	-	-	-	-
Alaska	-	-	-	-	-	-	-	-
Arizona	0	0	0	0	0	0	0	0
Arkansas	-	-	-	-	-	-	-	-
California	-	-	-	-	-	-	-	-
Colorado	-	-	-	-	-	-	-	-
Connecticut	0	0	0	0	0	0	0	0
Delaware	1	1	1	1	1	0	1	6
Florida	-	-	-	-	-	-	-	-
Georgia	0	0	0	0	0	1	1	2
Hawaii	1	1	1	1	.5	.5	1	6
Idaho	.5	.5	0	0	.5	1	.5	3
Illinois	0	1	0	0	0	0	0	1
Indiana	-	-	-	-	-	-	-	-
Iowa	1	1	1	1	1	0	1	6
Kansas	1	1	1	1	.5	1	.5	6
Kentucky	0	0	0	0	0	0	0	0
Louisiana	-	-	-	-	-	-	-	-
Maine	-	-	-	-	-	-	-	-
Maryland	-	-	-	-	-	-	-	-
Massachusetts	1	1	1	1	1	.5	.5	6
Michigan	1	0	0	0	1	1	1	4
Minnesota	-	-	-	-	-	-	-	-
Mississippi	1	1	1	.5	.5	0	.5	4.5
Missouri	.5	.5	.5	.5	.5	0	.5	3
Montana	1	.5	1	.5	0	0	.5	3.5
Nebraska	1	1	0	0	0	0	.5	2.5
Nevada	-	-	-	-	-	-	-	-
New Hampshire	0	0	0	0	0	0	0	0
New Jersey	1	1	0	1	1	1	1	6
New Mexico	-	-	-	-	-	-	-	-
New York	0	0	0	0	0	0	0	0
North Carolina	1	.5	1	.5	.5	0	.5	4
North Dakota	0	0	0	0	0	0	1	1
Ohio	.5	.5	0	.5	.5	1	.5	3.5
Oklahoma	1	1	0	0	0	0	.5	2.5
Oregon	-	-	-	-	-	-	-	-
Pennsylvania	0	1	0	0	.5	1	0	2.5
Rhode Island	0	0	0	0	0	0	0	0
South Carolina	0	1	0	0	0	0	0	1
South Dakota	-	-	-	-	-	-	-	-
Tennessee	0	1	0	0	1	0	0	2
Texas	0	1	0	0	1	0	0	2
Utah	-	-	-	-	-	-	-	-
Vermont	-	-	-	-	-	-	-	-
Virginia	1	1	1	.5	1	0	.5	5
Washington	0	1	0	0	0	0	0	1
West Virginia	0	1	0	0	1	1	1	4
Wisconsin	0	0	0	0	0	0	0	0
Wyoming	1	1	1	0	1	0	1	5
Washington D.C.	0	0	0	0	0	0	0	0

Data Collection Procedures: Evaluation Goals & Purposes
Indicator A: Does the state identify a goal or purpose for superintendent evaluation?
Data Collection Procedures: Selected Performance Criteria and Measures
Indicator B: Does the state mandate particular superintendent evaluation criteria or components?
Indicator C: Do the mandated criteria or components directly name any existing professional educational standards or reflect at least 75% of any existing professional educational standards even if such standards are not directly named?
Indicator D: Does the state identify evaluation components that specifically reference the goals or purpose for superintendent evaluation?
Indicator E: Does the state mandate inclusion of student performance measures in the superintendent evaluation?
Methods for Using Results
Indicator F: Does the state mandate or permit superintendent contractual provisions based upon evaluation results?
Indicator G: Does the state mandate or permit evaluation results to be used for development of a professional growth plan (or similar documents) or other human resource decisions?

Summary Rubric Results for the Feasibility Standard by State

State	Indicator A	Indicator B	Total Score
Alabama	-	-	-
Alaska	-	-	-
Arizona	0	0	0
Arkansas	-	-	-
California	-	-	-
Colorado	-	-	-
Connecticut	1	0	1
Delaware	1	1	2
Florida	-	-	-
Georgia	1	0	1
Hawaii	1	0	1
Idaho	1	0	1
Illinois	0	0	0
Indiana	-	-	-
Iowa	1	0	1
Kansas	1	0	1
Kentucky	0	0	0
Louisiana	-	-	-
Maine	-	-	-
Maryland	-	-	-
Massachusetts	1	1	2
Michigan	1	1	2
Minnesota	-	-	-
Mississippi	1	0	1
Missouri	.5	0	0.5
Montana	1	0	1
Nebraska	1	0	1
Nevada	-	-	-
New Hampshire	1	0	1
New Jersey	1	0	1
New Mexico	-	-	-
New York	1	1	2
North Carolina	1	0	1
North Dakota	1	0	1
Ohio	.5	0	0.5
Oklahoma	1	0	1
Oregon	-	-	-
Pennsylvania	0	0	0
Rhode Island	0	0	0
South Carolina	0	0	0
South Dakota	-	-	-
Tennessee	1	0	1
Texas	1	0	1
Utah	-	-	-
Vermont	-	-	-
Virginia	1	0	1
Washington	1	1	2
West Virginia	1	0	1
Wisconsin	0	0	0
Wyoming	1	0	1
Washington D.C.	1	0	1

Data Collection Procedures: Frequency of Evaluation
Indicator A: Does the state dictate frequency of superintendent evaluation?
Data Collection Procedures: Reporting
Indicator B: Does the state maintain a superintendent process data tracking system? (i.e., Does the state require districts to report superintendent evaluation results to the state?)

Summary Rubric Results for the Accuracy Standard by State

State	Indicator A	Indicator B	Indicator C	Indicator D	Indicator E	Indicator F	Indicator G	Indicator H	Indicator I	Indicator J	Total Score
Alabama	-	-	-	-	-	-	-	-	-	-	-
Alaska	-	-	-	-	-	-	-	-	-	-	-
Arizona	0	0	0	1	0	0	0	0	0	0	1
Arkansas	-	-	-	-	-	-	-	-	-	-	-
California	-	-	-	-	-	-	-	-	-	-	-
Colorado	-	-	-	-	-	-	-	-	-	-	-
Connecticut	0	0	0	1	0	0	0	0	0	0	1
Delaware	1	0	1	1	.5	1	0	1	0	0	5.5
Florida	-	-	-	-	-	-	-	-	-	-	-
Georgia	0	0	.5	1	0	0	0	0	0	0	1.5
Hawaii	.5	0	.5	1	1	0	0	0	0	0	3
Idaho	0	0	0	1	0	0	0	0	0	0	1
Illinois	0	0	0	1	0	0	0	0	0	0	1
Indiana	-	-	-	-	-	-	-	-	-	-	-
Iowa	1	0	.5	1	.5	0	0	0	0	0	3
Kansas	1	0	0	1	1	1	0	0	0	0	4
Kentucky	0	0	0	1	0	.5	0	0	0	0	1.5
Louisiana	-	-	-	-	-	-	-	-	-	-	-
Maine	-	-	-	-	-	-	-	-	-	-	-
Maryland	-	-	-	-	-	-	-	-	-	-	-
Massachusetts	1	0	.5	1	1	1	1	0	0	.5	6
Michigan	1	0	1	1	1	1	1	.5	0	0	6.5
Minnesota	-	-	-	-	-	-	-	-	-	-	-
Mississippi	.5	0	.5	1	1	0	0	0	0	0	3
Missouri	.5	0	.5	1	.5	0	.5	0	.5	0	3.5
Montana	0	0	.5	1	1	0	0	0	0	0	2.5
Nebraska	0	0	0	1	0	0	0	0	0	0	1
Nevada	-	-	-	-	-	-	-	-	-	-	-
New Hampshire	0	0	0	1	0	0	0	0	0	0	1
New Jersey	.5	0	.5	1	1	0	0	0	0	0	3
New Mexico	-	-	-	-	-	-	-	-	-	-	-
New York	0	0	0	1	0	0	0	0	0	0	1
North Carolina	.5	0	1	1	1	0	0	0	0	1	4.5
North Dakota	0	0	0	1	0	0	0	0	0	0	1
Ohio	.5	0	.5	1	.5	0	0	0	0	0	2.5
Oklahoma	0	0	0	1	0	1	0	0	0	0	2
Oregon	-	-	-	-	-	-	-	-	-	-	-
Pennsylvania	0	0	0	1	0	0	0	0	0	0	1
Rhode Island	0	0	0	1	0	0	0	0	0	0	1
South Carolina	0	0	0	1	0	0	0	0	0	0	1
South Dakota	-	-	-	-	-	-	-	-	-	-	0
Tennessee	0	0	0	1	0	0	0	0	0	0	1
Texas	0	0	.5	1	1	0	0	0	0	0	2.5
Utah	-	-	-	-	-	-	-	-	-	-	-
Vermont	-	-	-	-	-	-	-	-	-	-	-
Virginia	1	0	.5	1	.5	0	0	0	0	0	3
Washington	0	0	0	1	0	1	0	0	0	0	2
West Virginia	0	0	.5	1	.5	1	0	0	0	0	3
Wisconsin	1	0	0	1	0	0	0	0	0	0	2
Wyoming	1	0	.5	1	0	1	0	0	0	0	3.5
Washington D.C.	0	0	0	1	0	0	0	0	0	0	1

Data Collection Procedures: Data Integrity
Indicator A: Does the state mandate that multiple sources of data must be used in the superintendent process?
Indicator B: Does the state assign different weights to different sources of superintendent evaluation data?
Indicator C: Does the state mandate a particular form for the superintendent evaluation?
Indicator D: Does the state identify evaluators for the superintendent evaluation?
Indicator E: Does the state mandate that multiple evaluator sources be used in the superintendent process?
Methods for Summarizing Results & System Evaluation
Indicator F: Does the state mandate a process to assess the state-level superintendent evaluation system's effectiveness?
Indicator G: Did the state pilot the superintendent evaluation system model process or form?
Indicator H: Does the state identify outcomes to determine overall effectiveness of state-level superintendent evaluation system?
System Structure: Recognition of District-Specific Demographics
Indicator I: Does the state differentiate between type of district (e.g. rural, urban, suburban) in the superintendent evaluation process?
Indicator J: Does the state differentiate between any district demographics in the superintendent evaluation process?

Index

Please note all references to figures are italicized.

AASA. *See* American Association of School Administrators

AASA professional standards. *See* American Association of School Administrators professional standards

accountability: cry for, 28; as double-edged sword, 97; federal, 1, 34, 42

accountability movement: ESSA impacting, 34–35; reform Acts for, 14–16; state-level evaluation in relation to, 33, 56

accuracy standards: coherence with, lack of, 93; description and application of, *7*; rubric scores for, state-by-state, *211*; rubric scores for, statewide frequency of, 49–51, *50*; state-level evaluation criteria for, *40*; Stronge on neglect of, 53; types and definitions of, 10–11

American Association of School Administrators (AASA): for formal evaluations, 1; NSBA collaborating with, 19, 20; responsibilities defined by NSBA and, *22–23*, 23

American Association of School Administrators (AASA)

professional standards: AASA/NSBA responsibilities and, *22–23*, 23; competencies related to, *20–22*; domains relationship to, *61*, 67–68; indicators for, 105, *106–12*; key descriptors for, *67*; recommendations, 64

artifact analysis, 79

balance of transparency, 95

Bennis, Warren, 16

bias: accuracy standards and, 93; personality criteria and, 80

Board of Education: expectations of, expanding, 18; local, issues for, 52; policy sample, 199–201; procedures sample, 203–4; as public representative, 4; rating scale used by, 145; role and responsibilities of, 199–201; superintendent relationship with, 35–36; turnover in, 54. *See also* school boards

Carter, G. R., 67

Center for Research on Educational Accountability and Teacher Evaluation (CREATE), 26–28, *27*, *28*

state-level evaluation criteria for, *39*;
types and definitions of, 9–10
federal accountability: ESSA for, 1, 34;
state-level evaluation revisions and,
42
feedback: of community, as
representation, 79–80; for growth, 26;
rating scale for, 145; value of, 102
fidelity, 44–45
formative evaluation: implementation
schedule for, 92; state-level emphasis
on components of, 55
forms: community survey, *134*;
performance goal sample, *130–32*;
staff survey, *135–36*. *See also*
evaluation forms
four-level rating scale: purpose of, 145;
rating criteria and definitions for,
146; summative evaluation form I,
148–56; summative evaluation form
II, *168–75*; summative evaluation
form III, *180–86*; summative
evaluation form IV, *192–94*
frequency of evaluation: emphasis on
increasing, 55; state-level, 48–49

global judgment, 26, 27, *27*, *28*
goals: consensus of, 95; organizational,
5, 98; organizational skills for
achieving, 121–22; performance,
78, *130–32*; policy, 89; report on
progress of, 203–4; school district,
evaluations based on, 199; school
districts achievement of, 102–3; self-
assessment for future, 81; state-level
evaluation, types of, 47; of student
achievement, 101–2
goal setting, *77*, 77–78

Human Resources Management
standard: AASA/NSBA Professional
Responsibilities and, *23*;
competencies related to, *21–22*;
indicators, *111*; key descriptors
for, *67*

human skills: for effectiveness, 17;
professional standard comparisons
for, *70*

implementation: considerations, 63; of
employee performance evaluation
system, 123; policy components
and, 88–89; of procedures, 203–4;
reviews and monitors for proper,
94–95; schedule, 91–92, *92*; of state-
of-the-art evaluation, guidelines for,
100–101; timeline, 99, *100*; training
for, 93–94
indicators: AASA professional
standards and, directions for,
105; for Communications and
Community Relations standard,
107; for Curriculum Planning and
Development standard, *109*; for
Human Resources Management
standard, *111*; for Instructional
Management standard, *110*; for
Leadership and District Culture
standard, *106*; for Organizational
Management standard, *108*; for
Policy and Governance standard,
106; state-level rubric scores by
accuracy standard, 49–51, *50*; state-
level rubric scores by feasibility
standard, *48*, 48–49; state-level
rubric scores by propriety standard,
43–45, *44*; state-level rubric scores
by utility standard, 45–48, *46*; for
Values and Ethics of Leadership
standard, *112*. *See also* performance
indicators
instructional leadership: reinforcement
of, 71; for student progress, 24
Instructional Leadership domain:
description of, *65*; performance
standards and indicators for, 117–20;
sample performance indicators
for, *62*; self-assessment form
for, *140*; summative evaluation
form I four-level rating scale for,

About the Authors

Michael F. DiPaola, PhD, is chancellor professor of the School of Education at William and Mary. His teaching and research, in the Educational Policy, Planning and Leadership Program, has focused on the interactions of professionals in school organizations, formative and summative assessment of professionals, school improvement, and the preparation of school leaders. He is the co-author of two books, including *Improving Instruction through Supervision, Evaluation, and Professional Development* in its second edition. In addition, his research has been published in venues such as the *Journal of Educational Administration*, *Journal of School Leadership*, and *The High School Journal.* He has co-edited eight books and authored ten book chapters. Prior to accepting his position at the university in 1998, Dr. DiPaola's career in public schools spanned three decades. He has served as a classroom teacher, school assistant principal, high school principal, and district superintendent.

Dr. Steven R. Staples, PhD, completed his bachelor's and master's degrees at the College of William and Mary and earned a doctorate in educational administration from Virginia Tech. During a forty-plus-year career in public education he served as a teacher at the elementary, middle, and high school levels as well as an assistant principal and principal in high school. He also served as an assistant superintendent for instruction and from 1991 to 2008 was superintendent of the York County School Division in Virginia. He left that post to serve on the faculty of the School of Education at William and Mary from 2008 to 2012. During a time of challenging conditions for public education in the Commonwealth, he left the faculty post to lead the state superintendent's association and engage practicing educators in the policy-making process across the state. That service led to his selection as the state superintendent of public instruction for the Commonwealth under Governor Terry McAuliffe. During his service as the state chief, he led the reform effort in Virginia to reduce dependence on standardized tests and support deeper learning initiatives in classrooms. His retirement from the state chief's post in January 2018 allowed him to return to the faculty at William and Mary as a part-time executive professor.

Tracey L. Schneider, JD, PhD, is an assistant professor of organizational leadership (an Executive EdD program) at Stockton University. Dr. Schneider earned her JD from the University of Richmond School of Law and began her career in education as an education law attorney. For more than twelve years, she worked with school administrators and school boards to better understand and comply with laws impacting schools. She returned to school to continue her career in education law with a new perspective and to study the impact and influence of law and policy on education leaders. Dr. Schneider earned her PhD in educational policy, planning, and leadership from the College of William and Mary. Dr. Schneider's teaching and research interests include education law, professional learning and development in education law, education policy, law and ethics in leadership, and research methods. She travels throughout the United States to provide training and professional development programs to school administrators, school boards, and attorneys on a variety of education law and policy issues.

Lightning Source UK Ltd.
Milton Keynes UK
UKHW011526160819
348010UK00012B/162/P